THE PATH TO
PURITY

JEFF HARVILL

THE PATH TO
PURITY

gatekeeper press

Columbus, Ohio

The Path to Purity

Published by Gatekeeper Press
2167 Stringtown Rd, Suite 109
Columbus, OH 43123-2989
www.GatekeeperPress.com

ISBN (paperback): 9781642372267
eISBN: 9781642372472

Printed in the United States of America

CONTENTS

PREFACE

Writing this book has been a labor of love. There is a special place in my heart for Christians who are struggling to overcome sin but have yet to discover how to do so. God can work with people like that. It would be safe to assume that since you're reading this, you are one of those people searching for the path to purity. The fact that you want to be pure says a lot about you.

If you are looking for help with your struggle against sin, you've come to the right place. I want to show you how to find victory in Christ. It is my prayer that you'll learn the truths discussed in this book much sooner than I did. By doing so, the transformation process can be expedited.

I consider this book to be positive in nature. However, due to the widespread problem of pornography, I felt the need to devote an entire chapter to the subject. Please don't think this book is only about pornography addiction. It also addresses many common sins and how to overcome them.

I would describe this book as simple and practical. I wanted it to be easy to understand for the common person, and especially for young people. Yes, there are other books that are more interesting, scholarly, and elegant. However, I think few books are more helpful than this one. By the time you finish *The Path to Purity*, I pray that Christ will mean more to you than ever before. Thank you, and God bless you for purchasing and reading this book. If you have any questions, testimonials, suggestions, or prayer requests, please send them to thepathtopurity2019@gmail.com.

I

A PLAGUE OF EPIC PROPORTIONS

"I had a disease. I went to doctors and spiritual men looking for treatment. Their hard truths were not effective. 'Just stop! Don't do it anymore! You're a sinner!' Don't you think I've tried? I thought to myself. Don't you think I want to be well? Everywhere I went, I found new doctors who provided me with a glimmer of hope. *Maybe this one will be the one to cure me.* But all I got were the hard truths. Even within my relationships, those who loved me spoke the hard truths, 'If you wanted to stop, you would stop!' I was tired of being beat up by the hard truths. So, I stopped seeking treatment. I put on a brave face and pretended everything was fine. Outside, I appeared healthy, but on the inside the disease was growing. And it got worse.

"For the safety of others, I was placed inside a leper colony. I was sent to a place where the untreatable go. But my story doesn't end there. It was inside that place, I met a man. I had known about him for many years. I knew him to be a great healer, but I had never met him before. He drew me near. I knelt before him. I looked up with tears streaming down my face. I told him I was unclean. There was no need. He could see how dirty I was. 'Lord,' I said, 'If you are willing, you can heal me and make me clean.' Jesus reached out and touched me, 'I am willing,' he said to me. 'Be healed!' And instantly the leprosy disappeared.

> "On behalf of lepers here with me, and all over the world, we know we are sick. We've heard it all before. We don't need any more hard truths. What we need is for you to show us Jesus. Don't tell us about him. We know the stories just as well as you. But, we need to see him through you. We need to see the love of Christ through you. We need you to take him to us, so we can finally be healed."[1]

The article you just read appeared in a Christian magazine called, "Magnolia Messenger." I included this story to illustrate the damaging effects of a plague that is spreading throughout our society. No, the plague isn't leprosy. The "plague of epic proportions" is pornography. In the previous story, the writer uses symbolism extensively. The word "leprosy" is a reference to the young man's pornography addiction. The term "leper colony" represents prison. The young man's addiction raged out of control to the point that he broke the law and had to be incarcerated. Although his act of illegality resulted in a prison sentence, his life was changed for the better, for it was in prison that he learned how Jesus could deliver him from his bondage to sin.

We are quick to judge people who have the type of behavior problems previously described. We pass judgment on them, but aren't we partly to blame? It wasn't like he didn't ask for help. No, he was crying out for help! He desperately sought help, but no one knew what to tell him. That's where this book comes in. I hope to provide Biblical answers to those who seek help with pornography addiction, or any other sin for that matter. I want to show Christians, from the Word of God, how to have a pure heart, and how to have victory over sin. By the end of the book, answers will come. First, we need to look at how widespread this problem is.

You may be shocked to learn that the young man, in the story above, came from a Christian home. He developed a "porn" addiction even though he was raised by Christian parents, reared in the church, and baptized at an early age. How does this happen? Well, it may be happening because we're not teaching people how to have a pure heart. He obviously wanted to have a pure heart, but he didn't know how to be pure.

As I sit here writing, I don't know if there is a demand for a book on purity. However, I do know there is a great need for it. Pornography has spread across the globe like wild fire, consuming even Christians in its path. The statistics do not lie.

> 55% of married men say they watch porn at least once a month, compared to 70% of not married men.

> The following percentages of men say they view pornography at least several times a week:18-30 year olds – 63%, 31-49 year olds – 38%, 50-68 year olds – 25%. This next statistic is even more shocking: "64% of Christian men admit that they view pornography at least monthly." Finally, Proven Men Ministries reports that "Only 3% of

adult U.S. Christian males claim to
have never viewed pornography."[2]

Need I say more? These statistics sufficiently prove the addictive nature of pornography. Pornography has been around for a long time. However, internet access has caused this sin to affect more people than ever before.

Several years ago, I heard a story that opened my eyes to just how powerfully addictive pornography can be. I was in a work truck listening to a talk show on the radio. The topic that day was on pornography addiction. I will never forget what one of the callers had to say on that show. He said that he had faced three major addictions in his life: cocaine, alcohol, and pornography. Can you guess which of the three addictions was the most difficult for him to overcome? I was blown away when he said it was harder to give up pornography than it was to give up cocaine! That's how addictive the stuff can be, and the best way to overcome it is to never start viewing it in the first place.

Immorality of this type is nothing new to the church. The church has had a problem with sins of a sexual nature for more than 19 centuries. There was a scandal in the church at Corinth that would have made Hollywood producers blush.

> It is actually reported that there is immorality among you, and immorality of such a kind as does not exist even among the Gentiles, that someone has his father's wife.
> I Corinthians 5:1

The city of Corinth was a very wicked place. Many who had converted to Christ came from an idolatrous and promiscuous background. This man was having a hard time leaving his old life of sin. Paul rebuked the church for allowing the man to behave in this manner. He told them to withdraw fellowship from him. So, they practiced church discipline and withdrew from him. This was not an effort to toss him aside. Instead, it was a loving act, which was intended to cause him to see the error of his ways. Apparently, it worked, as God's plan always does.

> Sufficient for such a one is this punishment which was inflicted by the majority, so that on the contrary you should rather forgive and comfort him, lest somehow such a one be overwhelmed by excessive sorrow. Wherefore I urge you to reaffirm your love for him. II Corinthians 2:6-8

The world just doesn't understand how forgiving God is, or more people would want to serve Him. This individual was restored into a right relationship with God, and with the church, after committing an unspeakable act. This needs to be our attitude toward our brothers and sisters in Christ who have fallen victim to pornography. Those who are willing to repent of this sin should be forgiven and received with open arms. Many people who are addicted to pornography really want to change. However, they just don't know how to give it up.

If you feel that you are addicted to pornography, there is hope for you. It's a powerful addiction, but God is more powerful. Jesus Christ is our hope. In this book, I want to go further than just telling you to "stop sinning." You already know how wrong this sin is and how much damage it does to a person's relationship with God, and with others. I want to show you, from the Scriptures, how to receive victory over this sin.

But I don't want you to think that this book is only about dealing with pornography addiction. In the next chapter, we will see how a person can struggle with various types of sins. Nevertheless, the same Scriptures that help with pornography will also help with other sins. So, whatever your struggle is, please join us on this journey toward purity.

2

"WE ARE ALL SINNERS"

> For out of the heart come evil thoughts, murders, adulteries, fornications, thefts, false witness, slanders. These are the things which defile the man; but to eat with unwashed hands does not defile the man. Matthew 15:19, 20 (NASB)

In the previous chapter, we saw how pornography assaults the purity of Christians on a daily basis. If pornography is not a struggle for you, get on your knees and thank God. Our attitude should be, "But for the grace of God go I." We should avoid having a "holier than thou" attitude toward others who struggle with things that aren't a temptation for us. We are all tempted by something. What tempts you may not be a temptation for the other person, and vice versa. This chapter is written to remind us that we are all sinners.

> As it is written, 'There is none righteous, not even one.' Romans 3:10

> for all have sinned and fall short of the glory of God, Romans 3:23

We all need to pray, "God be merciful to me a sinner."[1] When we realize how sinful we are, we begin to understand how much we need Jesus Christ.

Certainly, pornography isn't the only thing threatening our purity. Jesus listed several forms of impurities in our introductory passage. Let's look at how our purity comes under fire from many directions.

For instance, greed is a sin that can threaten our purity as much as anything else. Greed doesn't get the attention and condemnation that pornography receives; however, it is just as wrong. The Apostle Paul said:

> For the love of money is a root of all sorts of evil, and some by longing for it have wandered away from the faith....
> I Timothy 6:10

Jesus said:

> No one can serve two masters; for
> either he will hate the one and love
> the other, or he will hold to one and
> despise the other. You cannot serve
> God and mammon. Matthew 6:24

The love of money can cause people to commit heinous acts. I once knew a man who was murdered because someone found out that he carried large sums of money in his pockets each day. The money, which he carried around, made him a target. The thief was eventually caught and sent to prison. However, his love of money brought unspeakable pain to an innocent family. Also, I've heard of people making the statement, "I would do anything for money." The Bible equates this attitude with idolatry.

> Therefore consider the members of your
> earthly body as dead to immorality,….
> evil desire, and greed, which amounts to
> idolatry. Colossians 3:5

The love of money has caused many people to lie, cheat, steal, kill, fight, etc. Yes, a greedy heart is an impure heart.

Uncontrolled anger is another threat to our purity. Until now, I may have only mentioned sins that aren't a problem for you. However, to prevent you from having a self-righteous attitude, I feel the need to bring you back down to earth. So, you don't have a problem with drugs, alcohol, porn, or greed? That's wonderful to hear! What about your temper though? Do you have a short fuse? Ever lose your cool? Do you find yourself "blowing up" and "going off" on people? Are you nursing a grudge against someone? Do you not realize that being a rage-aholic is a sin also? Consider the following statements from God's Word:

> Now the deeds of the flesh are evident, which are: immorality, impurity, sensuality, idolatry, sorcery, enmities, strife, jealousy, outbursts of anger, disputes, dissensions, factions, envying, drunkenness, carousing, and things like these, of which I forewarn you just as I have forewarned you that those who practice such things shall not inherit the kingdom of God. Galatians 5:19-21

Did you notice that "outbursts of anger" are listed alongside other sins such as idolatry, sorcery, and drunkenness? I encourage you not to take anger problems lightly. After all, anger made the list of things that will prevent one from inheriting the kingdom of God. Also, in the Bible, there are more warnings about anger than there are about drunkenness. In fact, there are a few striking similarities between drunkenness and anger. For instance, when people are drunk, they don't act like themselves. Anger also causes people to act differently from the way they normally do. Drunkenness causes people to say things they normally wouldn't say. So does anger. Drunkenness causes a person to do things they normally wouldn't do. So does anger. Drunkenness causes people to do things they will regret later. So does anger.

Also, research indicates that anger can cause heart disease, strokes, and high blood pressure. Anger weakens the immune system, and it has been linked to depression and anxiety.[2] Basically, uncontrolled anger is a slow form of suicide. God certainly had our best interest in mind when he told us to let our anger go. All of God's commands are for our own good. Later in the book, I hope to share some verses that will help us with anger. For now, suffice it to say, an angry heart is an impure heart.

Hatred is also a threat to our purity. It should only take one verse to convince us to take the sin of hatred very seriously.

> Everyone who hates his brother is
> a murderer; and you know that no
> murderer has eternal life abiding in
> him.[3] I John 3:15

The fact that God equates hatred with murder is enough to convince me to avoid hating other people. Notice that I mentioned anger before launching into a discussion about hatred. The reason for this is that anger always precedes hatred. Hatred usually develops after being angry with someone for an extended period of time. I encourage us all to love freely, pray often, and forgive quickly. This will help us avoid being consumed with hatred.

Before leaving the subject of hatred, please allow me to address a pressing concern that I have. I enjoy watching sports, especially football, as much as the next person. However, one thing that concerns me is the hatred that exists between fans, players, and coaches of opposing teams. I've even heard of intramural teams at Christian colleges developing a hatred for each another. Please keep in mind that the Scriptures still apply on the field of play, and in the stands. If it's wrong to hate someone off the field, then it's wrong to hate someone on the field. If it's wrong to hate a person, then it is wrong to hate a team, isn't it? Hatred is wrong anytime, and anywhere. Remember, the team you hate just might have a brother, or a sister in Christ, on their roster. Competition can bring out the best in people. But it can also bring out the worst in people. Let's not let competition cause us to hate our fellow Christians. Surely we can find a way to compete without hating the opposing team. Needless to say, a heart filled with hatred is an impure heart.

The final threat I want to discuss is lust. A person may be able to stay away from pornography and still struggle with lust. Out of all the verses in the Bible, Matthew 5:28 is one of the most difficult commandments to obey, especially for men.

"but I say to you, that everyone who looks on a woman to lust for her has committed adultery with her already in his heart."

According to this verse, God's standard of purity is very high. It's not enough to avoid committing adultery. Jesus is saying that we aren't even supposed to think about it. Jesus also says it's wrong to even look at another woman's body, unless she is your wife. I realize that many men will read that statement and say, "That's impossible." I would agree. Without God's help it would be impossible to avoid doing what Jesus condemns in this verse. The fact is, we do have God's help. In the Old Testament, Job, by the grace of God, was able to limit his attraction to his wife.

"I have made a covenant with my eyes;
How then could I gaze at a virgin?"
Job 31:1

Job was able to have pure eyes and a pure heart. By the grace of God, we can too.

If obeying Matthew 5:28 has been a problem for you, please don't give up. Help is on the way. You did not find this book by accident. For now, we are just talking about the problem of sin. I assure you, later in this book we will spend plenty of time discussing the cure for sin. Suffice it to say, a heart filled with lust is an impure heart.

This list of sins could go on and on. If I haven't covered a sin that you struggle with, believe me, I could have. Since we all need God's grace, we should be merciful and forgiving toward each other. Now that I have your attention, I want to provide you with some encouragement. Due to the subject matter, these first two chapters were hard to write. Perhaps, they were also difficult to read. I know that you're tired of being defeated by various sins, day in and day out. My goal was to motivate you to see a need for more purity in your life. When we feel that need, we will seek for victory more diligently. Please keep reading. God willing, the healing will begin very soon. If these first two chapters left you guilt ridden, perhaps some of the following chapters will lift your spirits and give you hope. However, we must first consider the consequences of our actions.

3

CONSIDER THE CONSEQUENCES

Then Judah said to Simeon his brother, "Come up with me into the territory allotted me, that we may fight against the Canaanites; and I in turn will go with you into the territory allotted you." So Simeon went with him. And Judah went up, and the Lord gave the Canaanites and the Perizzites into their hands; and they defeated ten thousand men at Bezed. And they found Adonibezek in Bezek, and fought against him, and they defeated the Canaanites and the Perizzites. But Adoni-bezek fled; and they pursued him and caught him and cut off his thumbs and big toes. And Adoni-bezek said, "Seventy Kings with their thumbs and their big toes cut off used to gather up scraps under my table; as I have done, so God has repaid me." So they brought him to Jerusalem and he died there." Judges 1:3-7

Adoni-Bezek had a twisted sense of humor, didn't he? He wasn't content to conquer other kings. Apparently, he also enjoyed humiliating them. He would cut their thumbs and big toes off to humiliate his captors, and to keep them subdued. After all, they wouldn't pose much of a threat without their thumbs and toes attached to their bodies. I wonder. Did this man ever stop to consider the consequences of his actions? Did he have any sympathy for his conquered foes? Was he ever remorseful about the pain he caused others? Probably not, until he got a dose of his own medicine. He looked at things quite differently after his big toes and thumbs were cut off. Now he knew how those seventy kings felt.

The Hindu call this type of thing "Karma." Others say, "What goes around, comes around." We Christians call it, "reaping what we have sown." Call it what you will, but there is no getting around the fact that sin always brings consequences with it. For every cause there is an effect. For every action there is a reaction, and for every sin there is always a consequence.

I know that many people question the Biblical account of creation, but I don't know how any sane person could question what the Bible says about the consequences of sin because it has been proven true time and time again. Think about this. If what the Bible says about the consequences of sin is true, and it is, doesn't it stand to reason that the Biblical account of creation is also true?

This is nothing to brag about, but I consider myself to be one of the world's foremost experts on the consequences of sin because I've experienced them first hand over and over again. Yes, I have brought many consequences into my life because of foolish, foolish decisions I made. It seems like I always had to learn life's lessons the hard way. I write this chapter because I love you, and I want to spare you from experiencing unnecessary pain in this life, and especially in the next. We have looked at several sins so far. The sins mentioned in the previous two chapters can cause so much pain in our lives. Considering the ramifications of our choices before we make them is not a permanent cure for our sins, but it may give us pause before choosing to disobey God.

I don't want to leave the impression that nothing good can come out of the suffering that sin brings into our lives. We can even see the grace of God at work in allowing us to experience the consequences of our actions. I remind us of the words of Jesus:

> "Those whom I love, I reprove and discipline; be zealous therefore, and repent." Revelation 3:19

Based on this verse, God allows us to experience the painful repercussions of our sinful choices to lead us out of those sins, and to draw us closer to Him. This verse also indicates that God hurts us in order to help us. You see, if we are having trouble giving up a sin, God will give us time to correct our behavior. However, if that doesn't work, He can send some consequences our way to provide us with the extra motivation we need to repent of our sins.

Young people, if you're ever tempted to drink alcoholic beverages, or to take other drugs, please consider the consequences. Alcohol and drugs can, and will, shorten your life by destroying your body, and your mind. You could get alcohol poisoning, or have an accident, or pass out, or get arrested. You could ruin your reputation and a promising future. Drinking/drug abuse could cost you a job, and ultimately your soul. It's just not worth it. You can have good clean fun without the stuff.

If you are ever tempted to commit adultery, please consider the consequences. First, you will get caught. There will be an overwhelming burden of guilt to bear. You could break up a marriage, or an entire family, thus scarring the children for life. I've also been around guys who had to pay a tremendous amount of child support. Therefore, adultery can even lead to financial ruin. And it can lead to further consequences, such as contracting a sexually transmitted disease, or even an unwanted pregnancy. It's just not worth it.

God forbid, but if you are ever tempted to take another person's life, for Christ's sake, I pray you stop and consider the consequences. Judgment is going to come on this nation, and it may have already started, if the murdering doesn't stop. I'm talking about the murders that take place on the streets, and in the wombs. As Christians, we need to remind people that one of the main reasons that God destroyed the world with a great flood was due to the widespread violence that took place during that time period.

> Now the earth was corrupt in the sight
> of God, and the earth was filled with
> violence. Genesis 6:11

One way or another murderers always get caught and punished, in this life, or in the next, or in both.

We could go on and on talking about the consequences of sin. However, I only want to address one more situation. If you are ever tempted to turn away from God, and to leave the church, please consider the consequences. Sure, you're free to walk away from God and his people at any time. We certainly aren't running a cult here. As Christians, we do have free will. You can walk away from the church; however, you can't walk away from the consequences of making such a decision.

The Prodigal Son tried going down that road. He took his Father's money, went into a far country, and wasted his inheritance on riotous living. You see, he never once thought about the repercussions of his decision. Therefore, he found himself in a miserable state of mind and body. In the same way, if we turn our backs on God He will see to it that we are miserable, until we return to Him. The Prodigal Son finally came to his senses:

> "But when he came to his senses, he said, 'How many of my Father's hired men have more than enough bread, but I am dying here with hunger! I will get up and go to my Father, and will say to him, "Father, I have sinned against heaven, and in Your sight ...."
> Luke 15:17, 18

If you have backslidden, won't you please come home? Return to God, and He will receive you graciously. You will be restored, forgiven, and treated as if you never left.

While we know the consequences that sin can bring into our lives, the idea is to live in such a way that you won't have to endure all the pain that comes with making sinful choices. I want to leave you with three principles that will spare you a lot of pain, suffering, and heartache.

First, a return to Calvary will prevent us from having to suffer many of the consequences of sin. The cross of Christ is very powerful. The closer we get to the cross, the less we sin. Therefore, we experience fewer consequences. Paul talked about the power of the cross in the following passage:

> For the word of the cross is to those
> who are perishing foolishness, but to
> us who are being saved it is the power
> of God. I Corinthians 1:18

The cross has the power to save our souls and to rid our lives of sin and its consequences.

God sure does work in mysterious ways. Years ago, I had a friend who had never seen the movie "The Passion of the Christ."[1] The movie was very popular back then. I went to see it at least once, or maybe twice, in the theatre. I also purchased it when it became available in stores. My friend, who shall remain nameless, wasn't a big spender like me. Instead of buying a movie ticket, he obtained a "bootleg" copy of the movie. Now, I certainly don't condone that type of behavior, but God did bring good out of the situation. You see, his wife was not a Christian, and she also wanted to see the movie. So, he took the bootleg copy of "The Passion of the Christ" home, and they watched it together. Well, she broke down crying as she watched it. She kept saying, "I didn't know, I didn't know" over and over again. I'm sure that she had listened to sermons on the crucifixion. However, the movie opened her eyes to the immense suffering the Savior endured at Calvary. The next Sunday, I'm happy to say that she became a Christian. That's the power of the cross! God is so powerful that He can even work through a bootleg copy of "The Passion of the Christ," and touch someone's life.

Another way to avoid many of the consequences of sin is to get back to the Bible. As we apply Biblical principles to our lives, we are able to avoid a lot of sins as well as the ensuing consequences. Notice what the Apostle Paul said about the word of God:

> And now I commend you to God and
> to the word of his grace, which is able
> to build you up and to give you the
> inheritance among all those who are
> sanctified. Acts 20:32

Surely, more people would study the Bible if they understood the many benefits of spending time in the

Word. The Scriptures can build us up, and give us an inheritance in heaven, thus greatly reducing the consequences we have to endure in this life and totally eliminating consequences in the next life.

I want to illustrate the powerful effect the Bible can have on our lives. Lynn Camp, from Amarillo, Texas, shares a powerful story about the difference just one Bible can have on a community.

"In July 1961, I boarded the Danube express at Vienna's West Train Station, traveling to Budapest behind the Iron Curtain. What a contrast between free Austria and Communist-occupied Hungary – so dark and drab! Businesses were closed. Signs were banned. People hardly dared to speak or smile.

Carefully contacting names accumulated in Vienna, we met Ivan Martos, an officer of the National bank of Hungary. He traveled to Vienna twice each year for bank conferences. Later, I arranged to meet Ivan at West Train Station. When he arrived, he looked like he had lost a best friend. Indeed, he had. Ivan related his bitter experience. Guards had boarded the train at the next-to-last stop on the Hungarian side. Checking all passengers, they came to Ivan. His ID and travel documents were in order. But one guard made Ivan open his briefcase. Finding Ivan's personal Bible, he held it up for all to see and angrily shouted, 'What is a man in your position doing with a Bible?' Before Ivan could respond, the guard threw the Bible out of the window of the moving train.

About two years later, at another Vienna meeting with Ivan, he was as upbeat as he had been downcast before. He had received a postal package in Budapest – it was his Bible! An apologetic note explained:

'Our children were playing one day along the railroad tracks. They found your Bible. Not knowing what it was, one of them took it to his grandmother, who immediately recognized it as a Bible. Word spread quickly through the little village on the border. Some of our older people had possessed Bibles before they were banned and remembered the significance and power of the Word of God. We decided to conceal the discovery while those who so desired would make handwritten copies. That joyful task lasted two years. Please forgive our keeping your Bible so long. But you might like to know that we are now a secret band of about 30 who have baptized each other and seek to follow Jesus in our daily lives.'[2]

Isn't that amazing? The Word of God hasn't lost its power!

Finally, we can avoid many of sin's consequences by judging ourselves. The Apostle Paul says as much in the following verse:

> But if we judged ourselves rightly, we should not be judged. I Corinthians 11:31

He made this statement after rebuking the Corinthian church for their abuse of the Lord's Supper. They had turned it into a drunken feast. Their hearts and minds were not focused on the crucified body, and blood, of the Lord. Sure enough, these sinful actions brought severe consequences into their lives.

> For he who eats and drinks, eats and drinks judgment to himself, if he does not judge the body rightly. For this reason, many among you are weak and sick, and a number sleep. I Corinthians 11:29, 30

Here, Paul is saying they should have caught these mistakes before the consequences came. We have to examine our lives from time to time. Judging ourselves involves an honest self-assessment for the purpose of identifying our weaknesses, and our mistakes. By judging ourselves in this way, we can seek God's help to correct our mistakes and to strengthen our weak areas. The idea is to catch our mistakes before we have to be punished by suffering the consequences of our sins.

In conclusion, while no one can live a consequence-free life, because we all sin, we can limit the number of consequences we endure by growing in Christ. This book is about spiritual growth. Considering the consequences, before making a choice, is a mark of a mature Christian. The path to purity is a path containing few consequences and many blessings.

Now that we have looked at sin, and its consequences, it's time to turn our attention toward forgiveness. I guess I've been like the military in these first three chapters. They tear you down before building you up. If I've torn you down, in the beginning of this book, I promise to build you up in the following chapters.

4

A WICKED KING MEETS A FORGIVING GOD

"Manasseh was twelve years old when he became king, and he reigned fifty-five years in Jerusalem. And he did evil in the sight of the Lord according to the abominations of the nations whom the Lord dispossessed before the sons of Israel. For he rebuilt the high places which Hezekiah his father had broken down; he also erected altars for the Baals and made Asherim, and worshiped all the host of Heaven and served them. And he built altars in the house of the Lord of which the Lord had said, "My name shall be in Jerusalem forever." For he built altars for all the host of heaven in the two courts of the house of the

Lord. And he made his sons pass through the fire in the valley of Ben-hinnom; and he practiced witchcraft, used divination, practiced sorcery, and dealt with mediums and spiritists. He did much evil in the sight of the Lord, provoking Him to anger.

> Then he put the carved image of the idol which he had made in the house of God, of which God had said to David and to Solomon his son, "In this house and in Jerusalem, which I have chosen from all the tribes of Israel, I will put My name forever; and I will not again remove the foot of Israel from the land which I have appointed for your fathers, if only they will observe to do all that I have commanded them according to all the law, the statutes, and the ordinances given through Moses." Thus Manasseh misled Judah and the inhabitants of Jerusalem to do more evil than the nations whom the Lord destroyed before the sons of Israel." II Chronicles 33:1-9

I remember when I first came across this passage. I noticed it as I was doing my daily Bible reading. I'm sure

I'd read this passage several times. However, the story never stood out to me. On this particular day, the passage jumped off the page at me. I was blown away by the wickedness of King Manasseh, to say the least. He was the leader of God's people. He was supposed to be a righteous man. Instead, he was the epitome of wickedness. His wickedness knew no bounds. Sadly, Israel and Judah only had a few good kings throughout their history. Manasseh was one of the wicked kings. In fact, he was probably the worst king of all, by far.

Think about what this king did. To start with, he was an idolater. However, he wasn't content with worshipping idols. He just had to bring the idols into God's house, of all places! I was also shocked to see a king of Israel involving himself in witchcraft and sorcery. And, by being in such a powerful position, he had the opportunity to influence people either positively, or negatively. Unfortunately, he chose the latter of the two options. He influenced many people to join him in worshipping idols, and in practicing witchcraft. His subjects probably thought this type of behavior was acceptable, because, after all, the king was doing it.

All the things Manasseh did were very disturbing. However, one thing he did was beyond disturbing. I was flabbergasted when I read about this man sacrificing some of his own children in the fire to one of his false gods. Unbelievable! Horrifying! Unspeakable! As a father myself, I don't have the words to describe how that makes me feel.

> And the Lord spoke to Manasseh and
> his people, but they paid no attention.
> II Chronicles 33:10

I mean it wasn't like the Lord didn't give this man a chance to repent. I assume the Lord sent a prophet to warn Manasseh and his kingdom about the repercussions of their actions. However, they chose to ignore all the gracious warnings God gave them. In the same way, God usually gives us opportunities to change our evil ways before he punishes us. God is so very gracious, and patient, in his dealings with us. Let's read on.

> Therefore the Lord brought the com-
> manders of the army of the king of
> Assyria against them, and they captured
> Manasseh with hooks, bound him
> with bronze chains, and took him to
> Babylon. II Chronicles 33:11

I saw that coming a mile away. It was bound to happen. As we saw in the previous chapter, there's a lot of truth to that old saying, "What goes around, comes around." Manasseh's actions came back to bite him. At this point, we cheer when the Assyrians enter the picture. Manasseh is finally getting what he deserves. He was acting like an animal, and they treated him like an animal. According to the footnote in my Thompson's Chain Reference Bible, those hooks were put through the nose of the king as he was led into captivity.[1] He was humiliated, and suffered tremendously, as he should have.

At this point in the story you are probably ready to shout, "Let him have it! Sock it to him! Pour it on him! Rid the earth of him!" I'm sure that few people would complain if the Assyrians tortured him 50 different ways. When I first read the story, I had some of those feelings too. Just when I was ready to raise my glass and propose a toast to the justice of God, the story took a turn that caught me completely off guard.

Before we read on, I want to make a statement that makes me a little uneasy. When you consider all the evil things this king did, it's hard to write these next few words. But, here it is. When you get to Heaven, don't be surprised if you run into Manasseh there. I'll bet you're thinking, what? How in the world? Surely not? I know. I know. The idea seems farfetched. But, the story isn't over yet.

> And when he was in distress, he entreated the Lord his God and

humbled himself greatly before the God of his fathers. When he prayed to Him, He was moved by his entreaty and heard his supplication, and brought him again to Jerusalem to his kingdom. Then Manasseh knew that the Lord was God. II Chronicles 33:12, 13

Isn't it amazing how pain, suffering, humiliation, and misery can change a person's attitude? When Manasseh was healthy and free, God didn't matter to him. Sadly, it took hitting rock bottom for him to give God his undivided attention. Some people just have to learn the hard way. I'm one of those people too. The good thing is, when you learn a lesson the hard way it usually sticks.

Judging by all indications, even though it was pain-induced, Manasseh seems to have genuinely repented of his sins, and he sincerely asked God to forgive him. Remarkably, the text seems to indicate that God did forgive him. These are the reasons that prompted me to make the statement about possibly seeing Manasseh in Heaven. God only knows.

So far, we have extensively covered Manasseh's role in this intriguing story. Now, I want to look at the real hero of this story. The hero in this story is God. In fact, this story tells us more about God than it tells us about Manasseh.

What can we learn about God from this account? Well, first of all, this story illustrates how merciful God is.

> The Lord is gracious and merciful;
> Slow to anger and great in loving kindness. Psalms 145:8

When God shows mercy, He does *not* give us what we *do* deserve. Manasseh deserved the worst punishment imaginable. Instead, God heard his prayer, forgave his sins, and reinstated him as king. Now that's mercy! If God was merciful toward one of the worst sinners in all the Bible, don't you think He will also be merciful to us? We deserve a Devil's hell, yet, when we repent, God grants us mercy. That's the kind of God we serve.

Second, we learn that God can forgive the worst of sins. The list of Manasseh's sins has been well documented. I will spare you from going over the details once again. The list is just that sickening. For this story to benefit us fully, maybe a comparison is in order. Take a few moments and compare your list of sins with the list of Manasseh's sins. Now, which is worse? I'm sure it's not even close. Manasseh was, by far, a worse sinner than you are. Here's the good news. If God can forgive this wicked king, He will forgive your sins also. I know we sometimes have trouble believing that God has truly forgiven us. Remember, God is willing to forgive any sin that we are willing to repent of.

Sometimes, the hardest person to forgive is yourself. We beat ourselves up with statements like, "I've done too much for God to forgive me." "I'm beyond hope." "God could never save a person like me." "I'm the worst sinner who has ever lived." These thoughts stem from a lack of faith in God's Word. When God says we are forgiven, it must be true. Believe it! Accept it! Thank God for His grace and move on! In order to heal, we must first forgive ourselves.

Third, this story teaches that God is a God of second chances. God gave Manasseh a second chance to be king. He made a royal mess of things the first time. He certainly didn't deserve to return to the throne, but God still gave him another opportunity. You might even say that God took a chance on Manasseh. Was there a chance that Manasseh could return to his evil ways? From a man's point of view, yes, there was. However, God knows our past, present, and future. God, through His foreknowledge, knew Manasseh was a changed man. That's why he was willing to give him a second chance.

Think of the many characters in Scripture who received a second chance. David received a second chance after committing adultery, and after committing second degree murder. Peter received a second chance after denying the Lord Jesus Christ. The Prodigal Son received a second chance after wasting his Father's possessions on riotous living. Yes, if we repent of our sins, as humbly as Manasseh did, God will give us a second chance. Sometimes we need a third chance, and a fourth chance, or even more. So, you see, it's not the end of the world when we mess up, if we are willing to repent. By the grace of God we can have a new start, like Manasseh, and David, and Peter, and the Prodigal Son, and many more.

I hate all the suffering Manasseh brought on others, but I'm glad this story is in the Bible. The story gives me hope. There are times in every Christian's life when we will entertain doubts about our salvation. This story can help alleviate our doubts and quiet our fears. Don't sell yourself short. Don't be too hard on yourself. If God can forgive a man like Manasseh, then He can, and He will, forgive you too.

5

IMAGINE THE POSSIBILITIES

Now after this, he built the outer wall of the city of David on the west side of Gihon, in the valley, even to the entrance of the Fish Gate; and he encircled the Ophel with it and made it very high. Then he put army commanders in all the fortified cities of Judah. He also removed the foreign gods and the idol from the house of the Lord, as well as all the altars which he had built on the mountain of the house of the Lord and in Jerusalem,

and he threw them outside the city.
And he set up the altar of the Lord
and sacrificed peace offerings and
thank offerings on it: and he ordered
Judah to serve the Lord God of Israel.
II Chronicles 33:14-16

The story of Manasseh just keeps getting better. If the events ended with him being forgiven and being reinstated as king, it would have been a great story. However, God was not finished working in this king's life. As the verses above indicate, Manasseh's repentance was followed by a radical change of life.

The story of Manasseh teaches us another great lesson about the ways of God. Not only can God forgive the worst of sinners, He can change the worst of sinners. If we compare Manasseh's character at the beginning of this story to his character at the end, it seems like we are reading about two different people. The man at the end of the story bears no resemblance to the man at the beginning of the story. He may be the same person on the outside, but he's a totally different person on the inside. The change is remarkable!

Notice the dramatic effect the grace of God had on this man's life. I'm sure he couldn't wait to get back to Jerusalem. He believed that things were going to be different this time. He had a second chance, and he wasn't going to waste it. He couldn't wait to rebuild the wall, which had been destroyed because of his transgressions. He made sure it was built very high to prevent further invasions. He went from being a bad king to a good king. He went from doing wrong to doing right. He went from being a murderous king to a preserver of life. He even posted guards to protect the people. By the grace of God, Manasseh made a 180-degree turnaround in his life. Another thing he did, which shows genuine repentance, was to remove the foreign gods from the temple of the Lord, post haste. Furthermore, he destroyed the idols and cast them out of the city, with great eagerness, so no one could ever worship them again. Also, Manasseh ordered the people in his kingdom to serve the true and living God. Yes, these were the very people who had followed him into apostasy. Earlier, he taught them how to sin. Now, he would teach them how to be righteous. I'd say the king made the most of his second chance.

This story should give us hope that radical change is also possible in our lives. Sometimes, when we are struggling with sin, we begin to think that change is impossible. The situation can become so hopeless that we think forgiveness is also an impossibility. Nothing could be further from the truth! The things that were possible in Manasseh's life are also possible in your life. Remember, we serve a God who can do the impossible.

"Ah Lord God! Behold, Thou hast made the heavens and the earth by Thy great power and by Thine outstretched arm! Nothing is too difficult for Thee," Jeremiah 32:17

"Behold, I am the Lord, the God of all flesh; is anything too difficult for Me?" Jeremiah 32:27

".... With men it is impossible, but not with God; for all things are possible with God." Mark 10:27

"For nothing will be impossible with God." Luke 1:37

".... The things impossible with men are possible with God." Luke 18:27

One of my favorite movies is *Facing the Giants*. At the end of the movie, we see the following verse on the Coach's mantle.[1]

".... With God all things are possible." Matthew 19:26

Although the movie is fictional, it does remind us of three possibilities. First, it's possible for a heavy underdog to beat a superior team. Second, it's possible for a couple to have children even though a doctor has said they can't. Third, it's possible to revive your career even though you were nearly terminated. Of course, as the movie indicated, these possibilities became realities after the decision was made to put serving God above all else.

In the movie, one dramatic scene takes place after Shiloh wins the state championship. In the locker room, the coach reminds his players of their accomplishments, and then he asks them, "Now, tell me what's impossible with God?" Each player answers, "Nothing coach."[1] After reading the story of Manasseh, and after looking at the verses above, I feel like asking all my readers, "Now, you tell me, what's impossible with God?" The answer I'm looking for is, "Nothing preacher." Believe it!

This book is about purity. In a few chapters, we're going to look at how to become purer. For now, I just want to convince you of the possibility of purity in your life. If we don't believe it can happen, then it may not.

If you consider yourself to be pure already, then believe it's possible to become purer. As the song says:

"Purer in heart, O God, help me to be; that I Thy holy face one day may see; keep me from secret sin, reign Thou my soul within; purer in heart, help me to be."[2]

While we can never be completely pure on this side of Heaven, we can become purer as the years go by. Imagine the possibilities!

If you can't surf the internet without staying off the bad websites, imagine the possibilities. Imagine being able to use your computer without having to use a filter. Now, until victory comes, using a filter is highly recommended. One day, victory will come and you won't need one. Just imagine closing your laptop, or shutting your computer down, and not experiencing any guilt whatsoever. Can you imagine all your searches being innocent, pure, or work related? They can be! With God, "all things are possible."

If you can't watch television, or movies, without lusting over the images on the screen, then imagine the possibilities. The programs on TV are raunchier than ever before. Even some of the commercials have turned into "skin flicks." Don't even get me started on the movies. You know how bad they are. The good news is, there are still decent movies being made, and there are still decent shows on TV. The problem is, bad images can appear so quickly on the screen. Imagine being strong enough that you can look away immediately. Imagine turning off the television, or leaving the theater, and not feeling guilty for having stared at all the unwholesome images. Through Christ, it is possible to look away.

If you feel that sinful thoughts are taking over your mind throughout the day, imagine the possibilities. Imagine, at the end of the day, feeling good about the thoughts you have dwelt upon. As the Psalmist said:

"Let the words of my mouth and the meditation of my heart be acceptable in Thy sight, O Lord, my rock and my Redeemer." Psalm 19:14

Imagine pure thoughts controlling your mind, instead of being controlled by sinful thoughts. I've heard people say, "It doesn't matter what you think about, as long as you don't act on it." Doesn't the verse above disprove that notion? Make no mistake, it does matter what we think about. Believe me, I know how hard it is to keep your thoughts pure throughout the day. We will look at how to keep our thoughts pure later in the book. For now, believe it is possible to have thoughts that are pleasing in the sight of the Lord.

If you are a preacher, imagine standing in the pulpit with a clean heart. Imagine being a man who matches the message. Imagine your thoughts and your actions matching your words. Imagine preaching and not feeling like a hypocrite afterwards. Hopefully, most preachers are living a pure life. Nevertheless, preachers are certainly prone to temptations. Preachers are not perfect. This book is especially for preachers who struggle with purity. If you are a preacher who struggles, imagine how strong you can be with Christ's help.

If you're having trouble being faithful to your wife, or your husband, imagine the possibilities. Imagine being faithful to your spouse with your eyes, and with your mind, and with your body. Men, if you learn to have eyes only for your wife, I promise that your level of attraction toward her will increase exponentially. You see, every time a husband looks at another woman he becomes less attracted to his wife. Perhaps Jesus was trying to protect women, and all marriages, when He said those words in Matthew 5:28. Imagine your attraction being limited to your wife. By the grace of God, it is possible!

Imagine overcoming sins which you've struggled with for years and years. Imagine breaking bad habits which have tormented you for decades. Imagine how different your life would be if those habits weren't hounding you continually. It is possible! How? Through Christ! There is victory in Jesus!

Imagine having a heart filled with love for God and love for people. Imagine not having any anger, or resentment, or bitterness, or hatred controlling your heart. Imagine how liberating that would be! With the help of God, this kind of life is possible.

Imagine having more peace, more joy, and more assurance of your salvation. As the purity increases in your life, so will the peace. As your purity grows, so will your joy. I have found that victory over sin leads to less doubt about one's salvation, and victory is possible through Christ.

In this chapter, I've listed just a few of the changes God can make in our lives. For some of you, these possibilities have been realities in your life for many years. You've lived a clean life, and your struggle with sin has been very limited. That's wonderful! Give glory to God. Others of us aren't as fortunate as you. For many of us, living the Christian life has been a mighty struggle at times. I ask you to be patient, understanding, and forgiving toward your brethren who aren't as strong as you are. Also, for some people, the possibilities described in this chapter seem like an impossible dream. Be patient. Keep studying, and you'll learn truths that will turn these possibilities into realities for you.

6

PROMISES TO THE PURE

" . . . . In the 1995 college football season, 6-foot-2-inch, 280-pound Clay Shiver, who played center for the Florida State Seminoles, was regarded as one of the best in the nation. In fact, one magazine wanted to name him to their pre-season All-American football team. But, that was a problem, because the magazine was Playboy, and Clay Shiver is a dedicated Christian.

Shiver and the team chaplain suspected that Playboy would select him, so he had time to prepare his response. Shiver knew well what a boon this could be for his career. Being chosen for this All-America team meant that sportswriters regarded him as the best in the nation at his position. Such publicity never hurts athletes who aspire to the pros and to multimillion-dollar contracts. But, Shiver had higher values and priorities. When informed that Playboy had made him their selection, Clay Shiver simply said, 'No thanks.' That's right, he flatly turned down the honor. 'Clay didn't want to embarrass his mother and grandmother by appearing in the magazine or give his old high school friends an excuse to buy that issue,' writes Walker. Shiver further explained by quoting Luke 12:48: 'To whom much is given, of him much is required.' 'I don't want to let anyone down,' said Shiver, "and number one on that list is God."[1]

Clay Shiver is proof that young people can make pure choices. Clay chose purity over fame and notoriety. This story gives me hope for the younger generation. Even though they face more temptations than previous generations had to deal with, many young people still desire purity. I've heard several young Christians say that they plan to save themselves for marriage. This is encouraging! Young people, we love you, and we aren't about to give up on you!

Before going any further, I feel the need to define purity. In any Strong's Concordance you will find various forms of the word "pure," such as purity, pureness, purify, and purifying. These words, along with the Greek words they are translated from, are very similar in meaning. In Scripture, the various forms of the word pure are defined as clean, chaste, innocent, blameless, consecrated, holy and clearness.[2] Therefore, having a pure heart means that sins such as lust, greed, pride, envy, and hatred are not controlling you. From a positive standpoint, a pure heart is one that is controlled by the Christian graces found in II Peter 1:5-7, as well as the fruit of the Spirit in Galatians 5:22, 23. In other words, to have the mind of Christ is to have a pure heart. This is the kind of purity that Clay sought. This is also the kind of purity we should seek.

It's important to understand that purity isn't merely a suggestion. Purity is commanded by the Lord. It's not something you can take or leave. It's not optional. As the following verses will show, purity is not something you can pursue only if you feel like it.

> Let no one look down on your youthfulness, but rather in speech, conduct, love, faith and purity, show yourself an example of those who believe. I Timothy 4:12

> Pursue peace with all men, and the sanctification without which no one will see the Lord. Hebrews 12:14

The preceding verse is very sobering. We are reminded that no one will see the Lord unless they are sanctified and holy. Yes, God's standards of purity are very high, and no one can reach them on their own. Remember, God's grace will keep us covered, and He will help us as we seek to live purer lives.

We should strive for purity simply because it is the right thing to do. However, if we need extra incentive, the Scriptures contain several promises to the pure. Purity doesn't go unnoticed by the Lord. God promises to richly bless those who are pure in heart.

"Blessed are the pure in heart, for they
shall see God." Matthew 5:8

The term "blessed" means "fortunate or happy" in the original language. [ibid] As your heart becomes purer, your life becomes happier. Obedience produces joy in our lives. Jesus is talking about a deep and abiding joy. In other words, this joy remains constant despite the changing circumstances in life.

After learning and following the principles outlined in this book, I can honestly say that there is more joy in my life. Several years ago, for some reason, I was stressing about speaking before a large crowd. The tension lasted all afternoon. It was so bad that I didn't know if I was going to be able to go on or not. Thankfully, the

Lord helped me out of a bind once again. On the way to the building where I would speak, I started thinking of the changes God had made in me (purity, love, Christlikeness, humility, etc.). In other words, I started dwelling on everything that was right in my life instead of thinking about the things that were wrong. As a result, I experienced an infusion of joy and peace that I hadn't felt in quite a while. Thank God, the service went off without a hitch. Yes, I can personally testify that purity and joy go hand in hand.

Second, God promises a Heavenly Home to the pure in heart. To "see God" means to have a greater awareness of Him in this life, and to live with the expectation of receiving a home in Heaven when this life is over. The Psalmist asked the question:

> "Who may ascend into the hill of the
> Lord? And who may stand in His holy
> place?" Psalm 24:3

The answer is found in Verse Four.

> "He who has clean hands and a pure
> heart…." Psalm 24:4

Yes, Heaven is a pure place for a pure people. Everyone wants to go to Heaven; however, the problem is everyone doesn't want to be pure. It's like wanting to be rich but not wanting to work. That's not a viable option. Several years ago, I used to listen to the Dave Ramsey Show on the radio. I appreciated his financial advice, and it was very helpful. He repeats a statement over and over on his show; "Live like no one else, so that one day, you can live like no one else."[3] He means that we should make sacrifices to get debt free, and to stay debt free, so we can have a secure financial future, which is very rare. We can make a spiritual application from Dave Ramsey's saying. Just as there are few people living debt free, there are also few people living a pure life. Also, just as there are few people who are financially secure in this country, there will be few people saved according to the words of Jesus. Obviously, we can't work, or earn, our way into Heaven. However, there are sacrifices to be made if we want to go there.

Third, God promises a clear conscience to the pure in heart.

> But the goal of our instruction is love from a pure heart and a good conscience and a sincere faith. I Timothy 1:5

A pure heart and a good conscience go hand in hand. We all have done things which have caused us to have a guilty conscience. The best remedy for a guilty conscience is to repent and receive God's forgiveness. I've also found that living a pure life eases a guilty conscience. The misery of a guilty conscience is lifted when we realize that God has both forgiven our sins and delivered us from sin's control.

Instead of following the plan above, many try to drown their guilt with alcohol, drugs, sex, etc. All this does is add guilt on top of guilt. Carrying around the crushing burden of a guilty conscience, day after day, can weigh a person down. Again, I can testify that following the path to purity will result in having a good conscience. When God cleanses your sins by the blood of Jesus, and gives you victory over those same sins, you will feel as light as a feather.

Also, God promises to answer the prayers of those who are pure in heart.

> Now flee from youthful lusts, and pursue righteousness, faith, love and peace, with those who call on the Lord from a pure heart. II Timothy 2:22

> For the eyes of the Lord are upon the righteous, and His ears attend to their prayer, But the face of the Lord is against those who do evil. I Peter 3:12

I find it interesting that we tend to pray more as we become purer. When we aren't living a pure life, we usually don't pray very much. But, that's precisely the time we need to pray the most.

I've had to rely on prayer many times in my life. God has proved Himself faithful over and over again. A few years ago, I found myself praying to God for assistance. On this occasion, I was working as an assistant teacher. It looked like I was in store for an easy day. Work was slow because the student I helped each day didn't show up for school. I was enjoying a relaxing morning. Suddenly, the phone rang. When I picked up the phone, the high school assistant principal was on the other line. He asked me if I could speak to the "Students for Christ" group who were scheduled to meet that day.

Normally I would jump at the chance, but the meeting was less than an hour away. I asked him how many people would be in attendance. He said, "Oh, around 50, or a hundred." He said there would be students and teachers attending. If I'd had a day or two to prepare, I would have loved to speak to this group. However, with less than an hour to get ready I was stressing out. I mean, I was at school with no Bible and no sermon notes. So, reluctantly I said "yes," and then I hung up the phone and began putting my thoughts together. I tried jotting down a few notes, but nothing came to me. I even tried to remember the sermons I had just preached a day or two earlier. That didn't work either. I was running out of time, so I bowed my head and prayed about the situation. I promise, within two minutes of ending that prayer, I had my topic! After praying, I knew I needed to preach on anger.

Now that I had my topic, it only took about fifteen minutes to prepare the lesson. I went to the high school and presented the sermon. It went so well that one of the teachers asked to make a copy of my notes. God helped me out of a tight spot once again, just as He has so many times before. Glory be to God! If, by the grace of God, you are living a pure life, take comfort in the fact that God has promised to hear and answer your prayers, according to His will.

These are just a few of the wonderful promises God has made to the pure in heart. There are many things that motivate us to want to be pure. The promises of endless joy, a home in Heaven, a clear conscience, and answered prayer should motivate you to seek purity like never before. Love the Lord, and let Him make you pure so these promises will be fulfilled in your life.

7

HOW NOT TO BE PURE IN HEART

In the movie, National Treasure, Ben and Riley were discussing how they could "steal" the Declaration of Independence. Of course, they were stealing it to protect it from the bad guys. Riley was trying to convince Ben that stealing the Declaration of Independence was an impossible task. Ben, however, knew there was a way. In response to Riley, Ben said "You know, Thomas Edison tried and failed nearly 2000 times to develop the carbonized cotton filament for the incandescent light bulb. And when asked about it, he said, 'I didn't fail. I found out 2000 ways how not to make a light bulb,' but he only needed to find one way to make it work."[1]

I don't know how accurate the Edison story is in the movie. There seems to be some confusion as to how many failed experiments Thomas Edison had. If you Google the story, the numbers will range from 1,000, or even up to 10,000 failed experiments. Also, there is some disagreement over which invention Edison's quote pertains to. Some believe he made his famous quote when asked about the invention of the alkaline storage battery.[2] However, one thing is certain. Edison's successful inventions were preceded by much painstaking research and by many experiments that didn't work.

There have been times in my life when I felt like Thomas Edison must have felt while trying to invent the light bulb, or the alkaline storage battery. I certainly wasn't trying to invent anything. But we were both searching diligently for answers. Edison was trying to invent things that would make our lives easier. I was trying to discover how a man can have a pure heart, and a pure mind, while living in an impure age. Both searches required much painstaking research and many frustrating experiments.

I became a Christian at age eleven. I experienced the joy and zeal of being a new convert. It was wonderful. I was on a "Hallelujah high!" Then, temptation came, sin followed, guilt set in, and I came crashing down. It can be horrifying when new converts learn that sinful desires remain even after being saved. It's also shocking to learn how susceptible to temptation we are as Christians. After dealing with sin and temptation, I didn't feel pure anymore. I wanted my joy back. I wanted to feel pure and clean once again. The search was on!

My search for a pure heart has led me down many roads. I was willing to try anything to be pure again. I bought and read many books. I talked to people who seemed to be living victoriously for Christ. Also, I suppose I've read Chapters 6-8 of the book of Romans about as often as any living person. Just as Thomas Edison discovered many ways to fail at inventing the light bulb, I've discovered many ways to fail at what makes me pure in heart. By describing some of these unsuccessful experiments of mine, I hope to save you a lot of time, energy, and frustration. My pain is your gain. By avoiding the same fruitless searches I went on, hopefully you can discover purity of heart much sooner than I did.

I was young. I was naive. I was just starting my walk with the Lord. When I first became a Christian, I didn't even know what some sins were. When I became more educated in the ways of the world, temptation started occurring regularly. I was woefully unprepared to deal with this situation. The first thing I tried was to fight with the temptations. I would try to suppress the sinful thoughts, or desires, that entered my mind. I thought all I had to do was block out any unwanted thoughts. Needless to say, this approach failed to produce lasting victory in my life. There are at least a couple of problems with this approach. First, it doesn't work long term. You can only suppress sin for so long; then it becomes stronger and defeats you. I found that out the hard way. Also, this approach doesn't work in our weak areas. For instance, if anger is your weakness, you will not be able to suppress it successfully each day. It will eventually get the better of you, because we can't overcome sin on our own.

As failure and frustration mounted, I turned to prayer. I would ask God to help me overcome sin. I also asked God to deliver me from certain temptations that were causing trouble in my life. While prayer is of utmost importance, this type of praying didn't seem to purify my heart. I've only met one man who had success with this approach. However, I'm sure there are others. Many years ago, a young man was telling me about the troubles he experienced while trying to give up smoking cigarettes. He told me that he prayed for God to deliver him from his addiction. Amazingly, he said the desire to smoke was immediately gone. I believe in God's ability to answer prayer. I'm not telling you to refrain from asking God to deliver you from your sinful desires and habits. He is certainly able. I'm saying that there is a better way to pray, and there are greater petitions that we need to bring before God. We will look at some things we need to be praying for later in the book.

As guilt took hold, I "walked the isle" a few times. I thought it would help to confess that I was a sinner, and to ask for the prayers of the church. Some call it re-dedicating your life to Christ. Others call it being restored to your first love. I call it getting right with God. Don't get me wrong. There was immediate relief from guilt. However, temptation kept coming back, and I kept failing. If you feel that you need to get right with God publicly, please do so as soon as possible. I just want you to be aware that desires and temptations will return at some point. This book is an effort to prepare you for those occasions.

At one point, I threw up my hands, and said, "God, you're going to have to do it." Up to this point, all my efforts had failed. So, I just did nothing and tried to leave everything up to God. Just as God didn't remove Paul's thorn in the flesh, He didn't remove my temptations either. I do understand that God's grace is sufficient. I believe that. I'm thankful for God's grace, but I wanted victory, and I wanted a breakthrough. However, I would have to wait a while longer.

By this time, I was getting desperate. You know the old saying, "Desperate times call for desperate measures." I was so desperate that I tried using a different part of my brain to overcome sin. It seemed like temptations were coming from a certain area of my brain, so I tried to avoid using that particular area when temptation occurred. Needless to say, back to the drawing board I went.

I can't remember specific occasions because it was so long ago. I'm only 99% sure it actually happened. You see, in another effort to overcome temptation, I recall using pain a time or two. Maybe it was pinching, or hitting myself, in an effort to become purer. I thought by associating temptation with pain, the temptation would no longer be appealing. Of course, I was wrong.

Apparently, I'm not the only one who has turned to pain in an attempt to become more spiritual. I've heard of people turning to things like shock therapy in an attempt to produce change in their life. Also, while doing research for this chapter, I came across a term called "self-flagellation." The Merriam-Webster online dictionary defines the term as, "The act of hitting yourself with a whip as a way to punish yourself or as a part of a religious ritual."[3] Surprisingly, down through the years, there have been some prominent religious figures who have practiced this form of religious discipline. I choose not to give the names of these people, or to give the name of the religious organization to which they belong. The last thing I want to do is to embarrass or shame these well-meaning individuals. I just think the practice is unnecessary, and unproductive. I only bring it up to show you another way not to be pure in heart. Apparently, those who physically hurt themselves are trying to get closer to God by experiencing a taste of the pain Jesus endured at Calvary. They may also be hoping to weaken their desire to sin by associating temptation with pain. I understand the logic, but there are better ways to be drawn closer to God. So, remember, no amount of hitting, or whipping, or shock therapy, or cutting, or burning yourself is going to purify your heart and mind. Once the pain is gone, the desires will return.

Certainly, as stated above, burning yourself is not going to make you more holy. However, I did know a man who was brought to the Lord after getting too close to a fire. This man was my father-in-law, Dallas Cooper. He was married for twelve years before he became a Christian. He was a good, hardworking man. He was a faithful husband, a loving father, and a law-abiding citizen; however, he wasn't saved. There had been attempts to convert him. One preacher was at his house talking to him about the Lord. I don't know exactly what happened, but Dallas told him to leave and never come back. The bold preacher said, "I'll leave, but I will be back." As far as I know, the preacher did come back later. His visits helped, but sometimes it takes a traumatic experience to get our attention.

As I recall, one day, as Dallas was burning some brush, he got a little too close to the fire. He wasn't harmed, but he did feel the heat of the fire. This event was a turning point in his life. He said, "If hell is going to be hotter than this fire, I don't want to go there." Shortly thereafter, he obeyed the glorious Gospel of Christ. It was a day of rejoicing for his family and for the church. Years later, he went on to become a Deacon at the local church where he attended.

While I strongly discourage you from burning yourself, it may be beneficial to get close enough to feel the heat from a fire, or an oven, or a stove. The next time you get too close to a fire, or a hot device, remember these words:

> And the smoke of their torment goes
> up forever and ever; and they have no
> rest day and night, those who worship
> the beast and his image, and whoever
> receives the mark of his name.
> Revelation 14:11

Think on this verse, and remember, Jesus died an awful death to save us from such an awful place.

After years of seeking, by the grace of God, I finally made a little progress. I came across a couple of verses, in the book of Romans, which had a dramatic effect on my life.

> for he who has died is freed from sin
> Romans 6:7

and having been freed from sin,
you became slaves of righteousness.
Romans 6:18

I would reflect on these verses any time a temptation entered my mind. I reminded myself that Christ had set me free from the power of sin. After doing this, I seemed to have more strength and more victory in my life. However, I would soon discover that I was only seeing one piece of the puzzle and not the complete picture. While it is true that Christ has set us free from sin's reign, it's important to understand how He has set us free. I was not there yet, but by the grace of God I was getting closer.

As the years went by, other pieces of the puzzle started coming together. I kept searching until one day I realized my life was forever changed. God didn't make me perfect, but He brought me to the point where sin was no longer "running roughshod" over me. With God's help, I was able to see four pillars of purity in Scripture. I plan on revealing these truths as the book progresses. For now, I ask you to be patient, stay with me, and keep an open mind. Approach your own search for purity with the tenacity of an inventor, like Thomas Edison. Don't give up just because you've tried many ways to overcome sin that didn't work. Keep searching until you experience breakthrough.

8

STUDY YOUR WAY
TO PURITY

It happened when I was around 10 or 11 years old. I was on a youth outing with our church at "Makin Music," on the campus of Freed Hardeman University. They really know how to put on a show. The music and singing were great! The choreography performed by the social clubs was mesmerizing. During the intermission, I went in search of refreshments and to look for a program detailing the night's festivities. As I was in line checking out, the cashier miscalculated and gave me too much money back. I realized the mistake as soon as the money was placed in my hand. However, I said nothing. Instead, I made off like a bandit. Knowing that I was about 15 dollars richer gave me a rush of excitement.

The next day, I was too excited to contain myself. I showed the money to my brother, and then I told my parents. Their reaction was not what I expected. I could see the disappointment on their faces as I revealed how I came into the money. Thankfully, I didn't get a spanking, even though I probably deserved one. Instead, they gave me a lesson in honesty, and then they told me the money had to be returned. My mother mailed the money back with an apologetic note. Nothing else was said until a letter came in the mail one day. The letter was from the President of the University, E. Claude Gardner! Brother Gardner said the actions of my parents exemplified honesty. After all, many people would have pocketed the money and said nothing, like I tried to do. Brother Gardner thanked my parents for returning the money, and he told them that he planned to share this example of honesty with the students at the college. So, if you've heard that story before, it was me! I'm the guilty party! It's a good thing my parents were there to correct me and to teach me an unforgettable lesson in honesty. That's what Bible believing people do. I'm thankful that I grew up in a home where the Bible was believed, respected, taught and obeyed.

In addition to making us honest, the word of God will purify our lives. Notice the words of the Psalmist:

> How can a young man keep his way pure? By keeping it according to Thy word. With all my heart I have sought Thee; Do not let me wander from Thy commandments. Thy word I have treasured in my heart, that I may not sin against Thee. Psalm 119:9-11

This passage shows the powerful effect Scripture can have on a person's life. As the Psalmist said, we have to hide the word of God in our hearts if we want to experience radical transformation. How do we hide the Word in our hearts? It's called memorization and meditation. We're getting ahead of ourselves a little, but meditation is a way to get the Word off the page and into our hearts. By hiding the Word in our hearts, we will be able to resist temptation in a powerful way, because the Bible will be controlling us. We have a choice. We can be controlled by the Scriptures, or we can be controlled by the flesh. Which type of person are you?

I cannot over-emphasize the importance of being a daily Bible reader. If we want to have a pure heart, we must become a diligent student of the Bible. Neither this book, nor any other book, can ever be a substitute for God's Word. In fact, I don't think this book, or any book, will help you much if you aren't committed to studying Scripture.

In Nehemiah 8:1-10, we see a people who committed themselves to the study of God's Word.

"And all the people gathered as one man at the square which was in front of the Water Gate, and they asked Ezra the scribe to bring the book of the law of Moses which the Lord had given to Israel. Then Ezra the priest brought the law before the assembly of men, women, and all who could listen with understanding, on the first day of the seventh month. And he read from it before the square which was in front of the Water Gate from early morning until midday, in the presence of men and women, those who could understand; and all the people were attentive to the book of the law. And Ezra the scribe stood at a wooden podium which they had made for the purpose. And beside him stood Mattithiah, Shema, Anaiah, Uriah, Hilkiah, and Maaseiah on his right hand; and Pedaiah, Mishael, Malchijah, Hashum, Hashbaddanaah, Zechariah, and Meshullam on his left hand. And Ezra opened the book in the sight of all the people for he was standing above all the people; and when he opened it, all the people stood up.

"Then Ezra blessed the Lord the great God. And all the people answered, "Amen, Amen!" while lifting up their hands; then they bowed low and worshiped the Lord with their faces to the ground. Also, Jeshua, Bani, Sherebiah, Jamin, Akkub, Shabbethai, Hodiah, Maaseiah, Kelita, Azariah, Jozabad, Hanan, Pelaiah, and the Levites, explained the law to the people while the people remained in their place. And they read from the book, from the law of God, translating to give the sense so that they understood the reading.

"Then Nehemiah, who was the governor, and Ezra the priest and scribe, and the Levites who taught the people said to all the people, 'This day is holy to the Lord your God; do not mourn or weep.' For all the people were weeping when they heard the words of the law. Then he said to them, 'Go, eat of the fat, drink of the sweet, and send portions to him who has nothing prepared; for this day is holy to our Lord. Do not be grieved, for the joy of the Lord is your strength.'"

Nehemiah returned to Jerusalem to rebuild the wall around the city, which had been destroyed by the Babylonians. Now that the wall was rebuilt, he turned his attention to rebuilding the lives of the people. Ezra, the priest and scribe, along with others, would use the Word of God to rebuild the broken lives of the people. Sometimes, our lives also need rebuilding. The Bible can rebuild anything that is broken in your life. Is your heart broken? Let the Word heal it. Is your marriage broken? Turn to the Word. Are your relationships broken? They can be mended by the application of Biblical principles. Has sin broken your spirit? Let the Scriptures renew your strength.

The Word of God had a powerful effect on the Israelites who had returned to Jerusalem out of Babylonian captivity. The effect was sevenfold. Your Bible can have the same effect on you as well.

First, the Word of God unified the people. They had gathered together as one man. There was no division, no competition, no fighting, and no power struggle going on in this crowd. There was only unity. The Bible transformed this divided remnant into a united nation. No other book in the world unites people of different races, nations, and backgrounds like the Bible does.

Second, the Word created a hunger in them. They had been in captivity for 70 years. They weren't able to worship, or study, like they once did in Jerusalem. They were so hungry for the Word, they begged Ezra to bring the "Book of the Law of Moses." That is so refreshing. Today, we usually have to beg people to come hear the preacher, but on this occasion it was the other way around.

The more you study God's Word, the more you will hunger for it. If I go very long without studying, I start craving the Scriptures. I remember hearing a missionary speak one Sunday. He'd been to Russia after the collapse of the Soviet Union. He told us about meeting a lady on a train. She was starving for the Word of God. She was so emotional, and so appreciative, when she received a copy of the Bible in her own language. She said, "Please preach to us. We have been without God for so long and we have no hope." How can we ignore God's Word, and leave it on the shelf to collect dust, when there are people in this world who are dying to read it for the first time?

Third, the Word of God kept their undivided attention. According to Verse 3, Ezra read for about six hours, and the people were attentive the whole time. They didn't have modern conveniences like air conditioning and comfortable pews, yet no one complained. The Word of God is so captivating that we can lose track of time as we read it.

Many years ago, a couple of men traveled a long way to hear a preacher. The preacher was very well known, and they looked forward to hearing him. After the service, the men started their journey home. On the way home, one of the men was visibly upset because they had traveled so far, and the preacher had only preached for thirty minutes, or so he thought. His friend told him to check his watch. After checking his watch, he realized the sermon had lasted for more than two hours! It only seemed like thirty minutes.[1] The Bible is the most interesting book in the world. When you are deep into the Scriptures, a few hours can seem like a few minutes.

Fourth, the Word demanded the respect of the people. According to Verse 5, as soon as Ezra opened the book, everyone stood up. Some writers have suggested that these people remained standing throughout the entire service. Either way, they showed the utmost respect for Scripture. Let's give the Bible the respect it deserves. To ignore the Bible is to disrespect it. To change the Bible is to disrespect it. To question its authority is to disrespect the Bible. To question its inerrancy, and to claim that it contradicts itself, is to disrespect the Bible. To say the Bible isn't the inspired Word of God is to disrespect the Bible. The lack of respect toward the Word of God in our day and time is a travesty. God expects better things from us.

Fifth, when the people heard the Scriptures being read, they responded with humble and heart-felt worship. In Verse 6, they were so stirred by the message they bowed their heads and worshiped God with their faces to the ground. The Scriptures have a way of stirring our deepest emotions. Many times, when studying the Bible, we are so affected by a verse that we stop and cry, or shout, or sing, or rejoice, or pray and thank God. Yes, the Word inspires worship and praise in our hearts.

Sixth, the Word of God convicted this congregation of their sins. In Verse 9, we see the people crying as Ezra was reading. The Israelites had been a rebellious people, and as a result, they suffered greatly. Perhaps they heard Ezra mention several sins which they were guilty of committing. Now they are sorrowful. Now they are penitent, and they seek forgiveness. The Scriptures should have the same effect on us. However, some people don't like being convicted of their sins. I heard of one lady who went so far as to cut certain verses out of her Bible. I guess those verses bothered her conscience too much. Or, maybe she wanted to change the Word to fit her life. But it should be the other way around. Instead of changing the Bible to fit our lives, we need to change our lives to fit the Bible.

Finally, Ezra's message brought them great joy. The joy of the Lord was their strength, and it can be ours also. They had a lot to rejoice about. In one day, they heard the Word, understood it, repented of their sins, received forgiveness, and worshipped God. No other book in the world can give you joy like the Bible can. On one occasion, I was talking with a Vietnam veteran. He told me he had trouble sleeping when he first came home from the war. He did not sleep well until he started reading the Bible every night. As he experienced the joy, and peace, and comfort of the Scriptures, he was able to slip off into the oblivion of sleep, and he finally got some much-needed rest.

If we want the Bible to have a powerful effect upon us, we must study it on a regular basis. It may take some getting used to at first, but once this habit is developed you won't be able to live without it.

In closing, I want to share a firm conviction that I have pertaining to the correlation between Bible study and purity. As I've already stated, everyone needs to study the Scriptures. However, I'm convinced that those of us who have lived impure lives need to study more than others. In other words, if you've sinned more than the average Christian, then you'll need to study more than the average Christian. Here's the reason why. Those who have been exposed to an inordinate amount of sins tend to have a more difficult time staying faithful. If we come from a rough past, we will face more temptations than other Christians face. To overcome those temptations, we must turn to the Bible. Thus, a great sinner needs to study a great amount of Scripture. May God be with you as you search the Scriptures daily.

9

YOU GOTTA HAVE A PLAN

> "I have found that my spiritual growth is directly proportionate to the amount of time and effort I put into the study of Scripture."[1]
>
> John F. MacArthur

Studying the Bible on a regular basis is so important that I've decided to spend two chapters on this topic. Every great servant of God has been devoted to studying the Scriptures. I can't think of a single exception. They didn't have a magical formula for success. They simply had a plan and stuck with it. For example, the Bereans were diligent students of the Bible, and they certainly had a plan.

> Now these were more noble-minded than those in Thessalonica, for they received the Word with great eagerness, examining the Scriptures daily, to see whether these things were so. Acts 17:11

These Christians were very studious, and very wise. Their plan was to test each lesson by comparing what the preacher said to what the Bible actually says, even when the preacher was the Apostle Paul. This was their daily practice. Today, way too many people accept what their preacher says without bothering to see if the sermon matches the Scriptures. This is a dangerous practice. This is how cults are formed. Recently, I watched three programs on three different cults. So sad. If the cult members had been like the Bereans, they could have easily seen through the devious plans of their leaders. If you are following a good plan for studying the Bible, the chances of being led astray by false teachers are greatly diminished.

Down through the years, I've met several different people who had great plans for studying the Bible. Not only did they have plans, they actually stuck with those plans. Persistence is the key. I hope these stories will inspire you to study the Scriptures even more than you currently do.

Richard had a plan. I remember walking across campus one day and seeing my friend sitting on a park bench. I could tell he was reading something, so I asked him about the book in his hand. He held up *The One Year Bible*.[2] I had never seen one of those before. He showed me how the Bible was arranged into 365 daily readings. The plan even carries you through the book of Psalms twice in one year. I was impressed. I was even more impressed when he told me that he was doubling up on his reading, so he could read through the entire Bible twice in a single year. I've used his method a few times. Each time I've read through the Bible in six months, I received tremendous blessings.

Billy Ray Adams had a plan. I'm not sure what his exact plan was, but I could tell he followed it religiously. Billy Ray passed away recently. He preached for many years in Alabama, and in Mississippi. At his visitation, his wife laid his Bible in the casket with him. It was worn out due to many years of continual use. His son called it the "Loose Leaf Edition." I don't know which edition of the Bible you prefer, but I think the "Loose Leaf Edition" is best.

My aunt Shirley had a plan. Shirley enjoyed reading many books, but the Bible was her favorite one. When she was sick, people would bring her books to read. She had a curious habit. When she sat down to read a book, she would skip to the end and read it first. If she liked how the book ended, she would go back and read the rest of the book. At her funeral, the preacher told the audience about her reading habit, and then he held up the Bible. He said, "Shirley liked how the Bible ended, so she went back and read the rest of it." The Word of God does have a happy ending. Go ahead, read the ending first if you so desire. If you like the ending, trust me, you will love the beginning and the middle too.

Melanie also had a plan. In Sunday school, when we were young, I was surprised when our teacher announced that one of our classmates had read the entire Bible over the course of 3 or 4 days. I'm sure her parents were very proud of her. This is not a plan we can follow on a weekly basis. However, I've heard of churches reading the Bible in shifts over the course of a few days.

Those pioneer preachers certainly had some great plans. Back in the old days, many preachers had to farm, in addition to keeping up with their preaching schedule. I've heard of some preachers who would read a verse of Scripture at the beginning of a row in the field. They would continue to quote the verse as they plowed the row. By the time they finished plowing, they had the verse memorized. Yes, the study habits of some of those "Old time" preachers were legendary. One brother, by the name of Franklin Camp, spent six hours in the Word each day. He'd wake up at 4 a.m. and study until 10 a.m. Then, he would spend his afternoons visiting and evangelizing. As a result, he had a powerful ministry. If we want to have a powerful ministry, then we need to spend more time in the Word.

My mother has a plan. Her plan is to read through the New Testament each month. This plan has worked well for her. It's helped her to be a good wife, and a godly mother, and a faithful Christian, for many years.

My friend Dan has a plan. Instead of reading quickly through a chapter or two, he may spend several hours on two or three verses. There's something to be said for going slowly through the Bible. Reading the Word slowly can help us retain more, and it can also help us to gain a better understanding of the verses.

So, suppose you're the type of person who just doesn't like to read. No worries. I heard of a man in Louisiana who didn't know how to read, yet he could quote volumes of Scripture. How did he accomplish such a feat? He memorized all those verses by listening to the Bible on cassette tape. It's amazing how much we can retain by listening to verses of Scripture on cassettes, or CD's, or on a phone app. Technology allows us to listen to the Bible while driving down the road, or mowing the yard, or even while jogging. Listening to the Word of God is a great way to learn Scripture.

So, you see, there are many different plans for studying the Bible. It's a matter of finding what works best for you. For what it's worth, there are a few plans that I follow. I make my way through the New Testament by reading a chapter or two each day. Also, my goal is to memorize at least one verse each week by writing it on an index card and reviewing it periodically. Additionally, I try to follow the plan in *The One Year Bible*.

Finally, this last plan has been so beneficial to me. The plan targets a broad range of Scriptures that will help us to become well-rounded Christians. I want to share with you a list of verses, along with their topics, which I try to read in one sitting a few times each week.

Psalm 23: The Lord is my shepherd	Psalm 91 – Trust in God
Psalm 146:1,2/147:1/148/150 – Praising God	
Matthew 6:24-34 – God will provide	Matthew 22:37-40 – Love
Luke 12:6,7,15 – Fear not, and beware of covetousness	
Luke 23:32-46 – Cross of Christ	Luke 24:1-8 – Resurrection of Christ
John 13:34,35 – Love of Christ	John 14:1-4 – Heaven
John 15:12,13,17 – Love	Romans 4:3, 18-21 – Faith
Romans 8:28 – Providence of God	Romans 8:31,32 – God is for us
Romans 8:35-39 – Love	Romans 12:10/13:8,10 – Love
I Corinthians 13:1-13/16:14,22 – Some of the greatest verses on Love	
Galatians 2:20 – Christ in us	Galatians 5:22,23 – The fruit of the Spirit

Ephesians 3:14-21 – Strength, Prayer, love, God's ability and glory

Ephesians 4:32 – Forgiveness

Philippians 1:21,23 – Proper view of death

Philippians 2:8 – Humility

Philippians 4:4-7 – Prayer is the remedy for worry

Philippians 4:13 – I can do all things through Christ

Philippians 4:19 – God's supply

Colossians 4:1-3 – Heaven

I Thessalonians 3:12/4:9,10 – Love

I Thessalonians5:16,17,18 – Joy, Prayer, Thanksgiving

I Thessalonians 3:16 – Peace

I Timothy 2:4 – Concern for the lost

I Timothy 6:6-11– Proper view of money, Christians should not love money

Hebrews 2:9 – Crucifixion of Christ

Hebrews 4:14-16 – Christ, our High Priest

Hebrews 11:1,6,13-16 – Faith

Hebrews 13:1 – Love

Hebrews 13:5,6 – God is with us

James 4:10 – Humility

James 5:19,20 – Soul winning

I Peter 1:8,9,22 – Love

I Peter 3:8 – Compassion

I Peter 4:8 – Love

I Peter 5:5-7 – Humility, Prayer

II Peter 3:9, 10 – The second coming of Christ

I John 1:7 – The blood of Christ

I John 2:6 – Christlikeness

I John 2:9-11 – Love

I John 3:1 – Love

I John 3:3,5 – Purity of Christ

I John 3:14-24 – Love, Prayer, Obedience

I John 4:7-21 – Love

I John 5:4,14,15 – Faith, Prayer

Revelation 21:4 – Heaven

The majority of the verses listed above contain wonderful promises from God. It's very important to make a conscious effort to believe these promises as you read them. I don't remember how I started this plan, but

I do know it has had a profound effect on my life. After reading these verses in one sitting, my mind feels clean and pure. This plan is so powerful due to the cumulative effect of such a wide variety of truths.

I can't tell you which Bible study plan to follow. I can tell you, though, that it won't be easy to follow any plan, because there are several things hindering us from studying as we should. Some people are hindered by a perceived lack of results. However, if we leave the results up to God, we will make progress. If you aren't seeing results from your studies, then study more.

Others are hindered by a lack of time. We all have busy schedules, but surely we can find 20 or 30 minutes each day to read God's Word. Also, some people quit studying the Bible because they think it's too hard to understand. Some passages are more difficult to understand than others, but we should not give up. We may have to use commentaries, concordances, or other tools. Of course, there's nothing wrong with praying for a better understanding of Scripture. Finally, sin can hinder us from studying. Please don't give up on your study plan just because you had a bad day spiritually. If you give in to temptation, repent and continue on with your study plan. If you fall flat on your face, don't make things worse by laying your Bible aside. Ask God to forgive you, and study even more diligently than you did before. Let failure fuel your desire for God's Word.

In conclusion, find a study plan and stick to it. Don't let anything, or anyone, stop you. You may regret doing a lot of things in life, but spending time in God's Word isn't one of them.

IO

BIBLICAL MEDITATION: THE FIRST PILLAR OF PURITY

The one thing I own more than anything else is books. Our house is overflowing with them. I love books, so it's only natural that I should write one. As I was preparing to write this chapter, I searched for a book or two on the subject of meditation. Sad to say, I couldn't find a single book in my library devoted to this very important subject. However, I did find some good quotes on the subject of meditation, which I plan to share with you. Here is the first one.

"Remember that it is not hasty reading, but seri-ous meditation on holy and heavenly truths, that makes them prove sweet and profitable to the soul…It is not he that reads most, but he that meditates most, that will prove to be the choicest, sweetest, wisest and strongest Christian."[1]

I agree wholeheartedly with the preceding quote. Before I learned to meditate on God's Word, I was, at best, a weak and anemic Christian. I'm thankful that God allowed me to learn the power of Biblical Meditation.

David knew the power that comes from meditating on God's Word:

> How blessed is the man who does not walk in the counsel of the wicked, nor stand in the path of sinners, nor sit in the seat of scoffers! But his delight is in the law of the Lord, and in His law he meditates day and night. And he will be like a tree firmly planted by streams of water, which yields its fruit in its season, and its leaf does not wither; And in whatever he does, he prospers. Psalm 1:1-3

In these verses, there are two key principles for victorious Christian living. First, we start by surrounding ourselves with good people. Our friends can make us or break us. Some have noticed a progression in Verse

One. Notice the order of the words: walk, stand, sit. Corruption doesn't happen overnight. At first, we are walking along casually with sinners. Next, as we become fascinated with their ways, we stand with them. Finally, as we are lured in, we sit among the scornful. This is why Paul warned us:

> Do not be deceived: "Bad company corrupts good morals. I Corinthians 15:33

The Christian who meditates on the Scriptures will not easily be led astray, and he will be less likely to fall in with the wrong crowd.

The second principle is seen in the fact that David was in the habit of meditating on the law of God, both day and night. The Word of God was on his mind constantly. This is the essence of meditation. No wonder he was such a productive saint. How did David come to be known as "A man after God's own heart?" The answer is found in Verse Two. Remember, David didn't have all the books of the Bible like we do. He just had the first few books of the Old Testament to study and to reflect upon. Living on this side of Calvary, we have the complete will of God revealed to us. Imagine how he would have studied, and meditated, if he had the Scriptures we have today. If David practiced Biblical Meditation, we also need to be doing it. We can benefit from this practice just as David did.

Notice the promises given to those who meditate on the Word. First, they will be strong like a tree planted beside the river. Also, they will be fruitful, and they will persevere like an evergreen, which keeps its color the year round. Finally, those who practice Biblical Meditation will prosper in everything they do, because God is with them.

Before we go any further, we need to define the term "meditate." The Strong's Concordance defines it as to "ponder, or to imagine."[2] According to Strong's, in I Timothy 4:15, meditation means, "to revolve in the mind." Therefore, meditation is when we dwell on, ponder, consider, think about, or reflect on a verse(s) for an extended period of time. Please don't confuse Biblical Meditation with other modern forms of meditation. Some religions have a form of meditation which involves clearing the mind of all thoughts while practicing deep breathing. Biblical Meditation is just the opposite. When Christians meditate, we are filling our minds with the truth of God's Word.

Christian meditation is becoming a lost art. We don't teach on the subject enough, myself included. As a result, churches are filled with weak, feeble, and defeated Christians. We can not live the Christian life victoriously without meditating on God's Word.

I can't remember a defining moment when I learned to meditate. By the grace of God, I stumbled across it. I think I just started repeating a verse in my mind one day. I was also thinking about the meaning of the verse and how it applied to my life. Soon afterwards, I could tell there was a difference in me. I seemed to have more strength, especially mentally and spiritually. So, I kept doing it, and here I am years later still going. One of the great joys in my life is to reflect on the Scriptures. I've been doing it for so long that I can't live without it. If I'm to be a faithful Christian, I must have a verse of Scripture on my mind, both day and night. Yes, I do think about other things too. Our minds are incredible. We can have two or three thoughts going at the same time. For instance, I used to watch TV and do my homework at the same time. Hey, I passed all of my subjects! Also, I know you can listen to the preacher and think about where you're going for lunch on Sunday. You shouldn't, but I know it happens. So, it's really easy to think about a verse of Scripture while doing chores, or watching TV, or driving down the road, or even while conversing with others.

I compare meditation to a steering wheel on an automobile. The direction the vehicle travels is determined by which way you turn the wheel. What would happen if you let go of the steering wheel and allowed the car to go in any direction? Obviously, the car would wind up in a ditch. The same is true of meditation. Just as we can't let our vehicle go in any direction it chooses, we can't let our mind go in any direction it chooses either. Both scenarios are dangerous propositions. Inevitably, our minds will gravitate toward sin just as an automobile will head toward a ditch. Let the Word of God steer your mind in the right direction.

Years ago, I worshipped with a man who prayed a beautiful prayer. Every time he prayed in public, he would say, "…. May the words of our mouth, and the meditation of our heart, be pleasing in Your sight." His prayer was based on the following verse which we briefly looked at in a previous chapter.

> Let the words of my mouth and the
> meditation of my heart Be acceptable
> in Thy sight, O Lord, my rock and my
> Redeemer. Psalm 19:14

As this verse indicates, God sees everything we meditate on. Imagine how pleased God will be when He observes our inner-most being, and He sees a verse of Scripture about His Son revolving in our minds.

As I mentioned earlier, there have been some great quotes on the subject of meditation. These quotes will give us a better understanding of what Biblical Meditation is all about.

"…. Meditation imprints and fastens a truth in the mind. Without meditation, the truths which we know will never affect our hearts."[3] Thomas Watson

Andrew Murray defined meditation as "Holding the Word of God in your heart until it has affected every phase of your life."[4]

"Meditate on what you read (Psalm 119:15). The Hebrew word for 'meditate' means to be intense in the mind. Meditation without reading is wrong and bound to err; reading without meditation is barren and fruitless."[5]

Based on the above quotes, meditation should be understood as mental digestion. You wouldn't put food in your mouth without chewing it, would you? No! Of course not! Unless food is chewed and digested, the body receives no benefit from what we eat. In the same way, the Bible is food for the mind. Christian meditation is the process by which our minds digest the truth. The more you chew your food, the easier it is to digest. Likewise, the more you "chew" on the verses you read the faster the spiritual nutrients will be distributed throughout your life.

One of the most challenging aspects of living the Christian life is dealing with temptation. When I first became a Christian, I didn't have a clue about what I was supposed to do when I was faced with temptation. Now, by the grace of God, it has become clear to me what I must do. I need to meditate on verses from the Bible, before, during, and after the temptation. I highly recommend that you do the same. In essence, that's what Jesus did when He was tempted. In Luke Chapter 4, He was tempted three times, and He responded three times by saying "It is written…." I'm so thankful that He didn't work a miracle or call down angels when He was tempted. Instead, He quoted Scriptures, which is something you and I can do. If Jesus turned to the Word of God when he was being tempted, don't you think we need to do the same?

Yes, some of the best advice I can give you is to silently quote Scriptures when you are faced with temptation. We have a natural inclination to try and block temptations from entering our minds. A better approach is to meditate on through the temptation. This means repeating a verse or verses relevant to the temptation you're facing, and think about the meaning of the passage, until the temptation passes. For instance, what if you are tempted to be prideful? We all know how sinful pride is. Instead of fighting with those prideful thoughts, try repeating (in your mind), and thinking about the meaning of James 4:10:

> Humble yourselves in the presence of
> the Lord, and He will exalt you.

Repeat the verse as often as necessary, until the temptation passes.

Let's go back to Jesus's temptation in Luke Chapter 4. After Jesus responded to each temptation with a relevant verse of Scripture, the Devil ended the temptations. However, Verse 13 says:

> And when the devil had finished every
> temptation, he departed from Him
> until an opportune time.

It's exhilarating when God gives us victory over a temptation. However, keep in mind, the temptation will return at a later date. Because we have the Word of God to meditate on, we can be armed and ready when temptation strikes again.

After defining and explaining what meditation is, I'm anticipating concerns you may have about implementing this practice. Some of you may be concerned about finding the time to incorporate meditation into an already busy schedule. Some of you also may have a job that requires your complete attention for hours on end. In that case, you may have to meditate during breakfast, or on your commute to work, or during lunch. Isaac's plan for meditation is a good one for busy people to adopt.

> And Isaac went out to meditate in the
> field toward evening.… Genesis 24:63

Isaac took a nice quiet stroll in the field to reflect on the things of God. I have found that walking and meditation go well together, especially in the evening.

Some of you may think meditation isn't any fun or may even be boring. Some of you may think meditation sounds like it would be drudgery. Let me stop you right there! I beg to differ. I can testify to how powerful and joyful Biblical meditation can be. Sure, it may take a while to develop the habit, but once you get used to it, meditation is quite enjoyable. Meditation is a way to become a positive thinker. When you meditate on a verse of Scripture, you are filling your mind with positive and powerful thoughts. Instead of thinking, "What if something goes wrong?" Fix your mind on the promises of God and think positive. Some may call this "thought replacement therapy." We do have to be thinking about something, so it might as well be the Word of God. Meditating on the Bible is much better than meditating on our problems. Meditation is enjoyable because it gives us so much peace, strength, and joy. Have fun with it!

I'm excited to have written this chapter. If these principles are applied, lives can be radically changed. In the previous two chapters, we looked at the importance of being a daily Bible reader. However, it's not enough just to read the Bible. We must think about the material we read. If you'll make a commitment to meditate on the Scriptures, as David did long ago, you should be able to tell a difference in just a few short days. The next few chapters will build on this one. Later, we'll get into the specifics concerning meditating on the right verses, at the right time, in order to receive the right results.

11

THOSE ANNOYING POP-UPS

I'm not very computer savvy. Slowly, but surely, I am entering the technological age. I can do the basics. I can send emails, write reports, and find the websites I need for the work I do. However, I'm still learning about trouble-shooting, installing software, and using anti-virus malware, etc. I don't like it when advertisements pop up on my computer screen, especially when I'm trying to get some work done. On one occasion, an advertisement from a company looking for inventors nearly cost me over 10,000 dollars. I had this idea for putting a beeper on a TV remote control, which could be activated from a port, so you could find it when it goes missing. You see, we lose our remote control quite often, usually at the most inopportune time. I was going to solve this common problem. They almost talked me into investing the money, but I declined and probably avoided a huge financial setback. On another occasion, when an advertisement popped up, I ordered malware protection from a fake company. I think they uploaded a virus that took over my computer. This all happened because the pop-ups looked so legitimate. Oh well, we live, and we learn.

Before making an application using the preceding story, I want to share another story. This story goes back to my high school days when I played football. I was an offensive lineman for the McNairy Central Bobcats, in Selmer, Tennessee. I rode the bench for three years before finally getting the starting nod my senior year. The event took place my sophomore year. As I recall, we were winning big, so the coach thought it was safe to put me in to play. I entered the game on a kick off during the fourth quarter. The other team received the kick, and I went jogging down the field. The ball carrier was on the other side of the field, so I knew I wasn't going to make a play. Slowly, I headed over to the area of the field where all the action was. I was still a good distance from the runner, when, out of nowhere, a player from the opposing team blindsided me. I never saw him coming, because I let my guard down. I was hurting, dazed, and embarrassed. To make matters worse, I had to watch the play on film the next Monday. When the coach played the film, he told the team to "Look closely at the bottom of the screen, and you can see Harvill's feet flying up in the air." The team had a good laugh at my expense. I guess it *was* kind of funny.

I wish pop-ups only occurred on a computer screen. However, pop-ups can occur in our minds in the form of a bad thought, or a sinful desire, or a temptation. I wish the football field was the only place we had to worry about getting blindsided. However, bad thoughts, sinful desires, and temptations can come out of nowhere to blindside us. If we aren't prepared for these dreadful moments, they can wreak havoc on our relationship with God, and with others. There is hope. The frequency and intensity of these unwanted thoughts will decrease as we devote ourselves to prayer, Bible study, and meditation.

Allow me to put your mind at ease. I know it's very frustrating when you're minding your own business and not looking for any trouble, yet an unwanted thought appears out of nowhere and tries to take over your mind. Trust me. This type of thing happens to all Christians. As far as I know, when a sinful thought first pops up, you haven't sinned. At that point, it should be classified as a temptation. It can't be wrong to be tempted because Jesus faced temptation also.

Now, if we go looking for temptation that's a different matter. No, I don't think sin occurs when unwanted thoughts first appear. What we do right after a sinful desire appears is very critical. If we dwell on those thoughts, certainly, we have sinned. There's a lot of truth to that old saying, "We can't stop the birds from flying over our heads, but we can keep them from building a nest in our hair." We may not be able to stop those unwanted thoughts from entering our minds, but with God's help, there is a way to keep them from remaining in our minds. We can't have a pure heart unless we learn how to deal with unwanted thoughts.

The question is, what causes these bad thoughts to pop up out of nowhere? What causes us to be blindsided by sinful desires? Well, before answering those questions, I want to mention a few ways that we can reduce the number of pop-ups. We can reduce these episodes by staying away from people, places, and things that tempt us. Also, these unwanted thoughts will occur less often if we are careful about the movies we watch, and the music we listen to, as well as the websites we visit. Additionally, as we mentioned earlier, you will be blindsided less often if you pray and study the Bible regularly. Following these principles will reduce the number of unwanted thoughts, but we'll never get to the point where our minds are pop-up free. So, we have to search for the root cause of our sinful desires.

Paul, in Romans Chapter Seven, will help us to understand why we are blindsided by various temptations. First, we need to understand that sin dwells in each and every one of us, even though we are Christians. Paul mentions this truth three times in the chapter under consideration.

> So now, no longer am I the one doing it, but sin which indwells me. Verse 17

> But if I am doing the very thing I do not wish, I am no longer the one doing it, but sin which dwells in me. Verse 20

> I find then the principle that evil is present in me, the one who wishes to do good. Verse 21

In these verses, it seems that sin is depicted as an entity that lives in us and tries to control us. So, let's put the blame where it belongs. Sin is responsible for the desires, temptations, and unwanted thoughts that we have to deal with. However, this chapter is enlightening, because it shows us how sin produces the pop-ups at the most inopportune moments. Paul tells us that sin has ammunition to use against us to get us to do the very things we hate. Sin is so deceptive that it can take something good and use it against us as a weapon. Herein lies a paradox. Sin is bad, but the ammunition it uses is good. The primary weapon sin uses against us is the law. Yes, sin uses the moral law of God to excite our passions, to create temptations, to create sinful thoughts, and to defeat us. Paul states this fact, as plain as day, in four different verses.

> For while we were in the flesh, the sinful passions, which were aroused by the Law, were at work in the members of our body to bear fruit for death. Verse 5

> But sin, taking opportunity through the commandment, produced in me coveting of every kind…. Verse 8

> …for sin, taking opportunity through the commandment, deceived me, and through it killed me. Verse 11

> Therefore, did that which is good become a cause of death for me? May it never be! Rather, it was sin, in order that it might be shown to be sin by effecting my death THROUGH THAT WHICH IS GOOD, (emphasis mine)

that through the commandment sin
might become utterly sinful. Verse 13

Have I said that the law is *good*? Yes, I thought so. I just don't want to be misunderstood. I love the law of God! The problem is, the law can't control sin in our lives. In fact, through no fault of its own, the law can make sin even stronger. How else do you explain Paul's statement in I Corinthians 15:56? "….and the power of sin is the law."

You see, when we try to use the law to deal with sin in our lives, inadvertently, we set off a chain reaction. First, when law meets sin our desires explode with intensity, and they can even rage out of control. Then the pop-ups happen. Then we are blindsided by temptation. Finally, we are defeated.

Maybe a couple of illustrations will help us understand this concept a little better. Have you ever poured lighter fluid, or gasoline, on a small fire? You know what happens. Well, when law meets sin, it's like pouring gasoline on a fire. The gasoline causes the fire to burn stronger just as the law causes our desires to become stronger. I reiterate, the law is not at fault here. It only has this effect upon us because we are so weak and sinful.

Parents, have you ever told your children they couldn't have a cookie before supper time? You know the effect that rule has on them. It causes them to want a cookie even more. The law has a similar effect, causing us to desire sin even more. For example, in Romans Chapter 7, Paul referred to a time when he tried to keep the commandment, "You shall not covet." Covetous desires started popping up in his mind, thus causing him to do the very thing he was trying to avoid.

Now that we are aware of the ammunition sin uses against us, we can begin to understand one of the main reasons God set us free from the law. The question is, how do we use this truth to our advantage? I have good news for you. One of the most difficult doctrines to understand (freedom from the law), and to explain, has turned out to be one of the most helpful and practical doctrines in all of God's Word.

Think about this. How would you feel if someone pointed a loaded gun at you? Any sane person would be terrified in that situation. Now, how would you feel if you knew the gun was unloaded? Hardly scared at all, right? Well, when we claim our Christian liberty, we are removing the ammunition from the primary weapon sin uses against us, the law. Without having the law as a weapon, sin can't cause our desires to rage out of control. In other words, if trying to keep the law excites our sinful desires, then freedom from the law should greatly weaken our desires. If our desire for sin is weakened, or removed all together, then the battle is half won!

Therefore, this information should revolutionize how we handle temptation. When a desire pops up in our mind, our first inclination is to fight, block, and suppress it. By the way, that approach is what I call "law keeping." For future reference, when I refer to Christian Liberty, or the fact that we aren't under the law, I'm referring to how God has set us free from having to fight, block, and suppress sin, with our own power, in order to stand justified before Him. God has given us a better and more effective way of dealing with sin and temptation.

Remember, each chapter in this book builds on the previous one. In the previous chapter, we looked at the importance of meditating on God's Word when we are faced with temptation. In this chapter, we identify specific verses to meditate on when temptation strikes. Therefore, when blindsided by temptation, we should meditate on verses pertaining to our freedom from the law. Here are a few verses to reflect on:

> ...by the works of the Law no flesh will be justified in His sight....
> Romans 3:20

> ...You... were made to die to the Law through the body of Christ...
> Romans 7:4

realizing the fact that law is not made
for a righteous man …. I Timothy 1:9

… for apart from the Law, sin is dead.
Romans 7:8

The preceding verses will be elaborated on later in the book. For now, try to commit the previous verses to memory so they can be used during seasons of temptation. As we meditate on these verses, we are reminding ourselves to avoid trying to fight, block, and suppress sin, on our own. Keep in mind, if we fight with sin it will only get stronger, according to Romans Chapter 7. We are also quoting these verses, silently, to take away sin's ammunition. Since sin uses the law to excite our sinful passions, claiming our freedom from the law should have the opposite effect on our desires. If the verses listed above are repeated by faith, with understanding, and out of love for God, the pop-ups should be stopped in their tracks. Also, those unwanted thoughts that blindsided you should go away.

Before leaving this chapter, I want to make one thing abundantly clear. Christian Liberty is not to be confused with lawlessness. Lawlessness is when a person chooses to sin with reckless abandon without any regard for God, or man. Lawlessness is when a person lives however they want to live. Lawlessness takes place when someone shakes their fist at God and defies all of His commandments. On the other hand, Christian Liberty is designed to kill our desire for sin, so that we can better serve God. The doctrine of Christian Liberty, properly understood and applied, will help us to become more righteous than ever before.

In conclusion, there may be some of you who are trying to fight, block, and suppress, unwanted sinful thoughts. Perhaps you have experienced more failure than success. I feel your pain. Isn't it time to try a different approach? To reiterate, fighting with sinful desires will only make them stronger. You can greatly weaken or even eliminate those desires by reflecting on verses pertaining to our Christian liberty. However, when a desire is killed in this way, it will return sometime later, and the process will have to be repeated. I know this concept can be difficult to understand, but it truly *is* life changing. Because Christian liberty is such a difficult truth to grasp, we will devote two more chapters to this subject. Stay with me. Please, hear me out. Keep an open mind. This truth can set you free from the torment of being controlled by sinful, unwanted thoughts.

12

THE SECOND PILLAR OF PURITY: CHRISTIAN LIBERTY

For many years, the verses I'm about to list, concerning Christian liberty, confused me a great deal. Even though I didn't understand them, I would read them over and over. It was frustrating, to say the least. I suppose it was easier to determine what these verses didn't mean. When I read the verses that said we aren't under the law, I knew Paul was not saying that we have a license to sin. That much was certain. I'd read these verses and walk away saying, "I'm not sure what he means, but I'm certain he isn't saying it's alright to sin now that we aren't under the law." I knew what he wasn't saying. However, it would take a few more years to understand what he *was* saying. Here are a few verses pertaining to our Christian liberty.

> …because by the works of the Law no flesh will be justified in His sight; for through the law comes the knowledge of sin. Romans 3:20

> But now apart from the Law, the righteousness of God has been manifested, being witnessed by the Law and the Prophets,… Romans 3:21

> For sin shall not be master over you, for you are not under law, but under grace. Romans 6:14

> Therefore, my brethren, you also were made to die to the Law through the body of Christ, that you might be joined to another, to Him who was raised from the dead, that we might bear fruit for God. Romans 7:4

> I do not nullify the grace of God; for if righteousness comes through the Law,

then Christ died needlessly. Galatians 2:21

Therefore the Law has become our tutor to lead us to Christ, that we may be justified by faith. But now that faith has come, we are no longer under a tutor. Galatians 3:24, 25

…realizing the fact that law is not made for a righteous man, but for those who are lawless and rebellious, for the ungodly and sinners, for the unholy and profane, for those who kill their fathers or mothers, for murderers. I Timothy 1:9

I don't want to pretend to know everything about these verses. However, there are a few lessons that stand out. First, we see one of the primary purposes of the law. The law teaches us what sin is. The law still needs to be taught because each generation needs to learn what actions are condemned by the Lord. Remember, the law merely points out our sins, but it takes the blood of Christ to wash our sins away. Also, sin is no longer our master, because we are not under the law. In the last chapter we learned how this works. By setting us free from the law, God took away sin's primary weapon, the law, which was used to arouse our sinful passions. The statement, "…the law is not made for a righteous man" is very interesting. Is he saying a righteous man is free to do as he pleases? Absolutely not! Instead, he is saying that you don't have to tell a righteous man not to steal, or kill, or covet, or commit adultery, or bear false witness, because his character is already changed to the point that he doesn't do those things.

I think I understood the implications of this truth pertaining to salvation, and worship. However, I failed to see how this truth applies to sanctification. Yes, I must confess, I didn't know what to do with these verses for a long time. To make matters worse, I had to teach about these verses from time to time. I remember one occasion. I was stressing out as I taught through the book of Romans. The first few chapters went well. But I knew that Chapters Six through Eight were rapidly approaching. I wanted to be able to explain these verses, but I didn't feel prepared to discuss them. I'd been contemplating these verses and praying for a better understanding of them for several years. Finally, by the grace of God there was a breakthrough, just in the nick of time, I might add.

I remember the event like it was yesterday. I was driving my work truck down the road about lunch time. Our class on Romans was only a few days away, so I had several verses on my mind. I was a little hungry, so I leaned over and reached into my lunch box. As I raised up, with food in hand, a wave of understanding came over me, hitting me like a ton of bricks. It was like a light bulb came on in my mind, and I knew my life would never be the same. I shouldn't have been surprised. After all, Jesus did say:

"Ask and it will be given to you; seek, and you will find; knock, and it will be opened to you." Matthew 7:7

My soul was thrilled, and I was so thankful to God.

Here is what dawned on me that day in the truck. When Paul talks about our freedom from the law, he's not giving us a license to sin. Instead, he is talking about a different way of becoming righteous! Yes, God has given us a new, and better, and more effective way of dealing with sin and temptation. Christlikeness apart from law is what the Holy Spirit, through Paul, is getting at in Romans Six through Eight. Of course! It all makes sense now. Instead of trying to fight, block, and suppress sin, i.e. keeping the law, God wants me to focus on the purity and righteousness of His Son, Jesus Christ. As a result, His purity and righteousness control my life, and as I become more like Him, sin isn't nearly the problem it once was.

In order to further explain this wonderful truth, allow me to use an illustration from baseball. Hank Aaron is considered to be one of the greatest baseball players of all time. However, he had to be taught to hold the bat differently from the way he was accustomed to holding it. You see, Hank Aaron used to hit cross-handed. As a right-handed hitter, he should have held the bat with his right hand over his left hand. Instead, he held the bat with his left hand over his right hand. Somehow, he still hit the ball with power. Eventually he signed with the Boston Braves. He was sent to the Eau Claire Bears of the Braves Class C farm team in Wisconsin. The hitting coach for the Bears convinced Hank to hold the bat the correct way, and the rest is history.[1]

In a similar fashion, Paul is telling us to deal with temptation a different way. He's telling us to look to Jesus instead of trying to overcome sin on our own. When we change our approach to becoming righteous, from fighting with sin to focusing on Christ, we become a purer Christian.

I may be getting too personal with this next story, but it will be worth it if someone's life is changed. Also, I share this story to show you how powerfully these truths can purify our hearts and minds.

I don't know if the place is still there or not, but it used to be called Alabama Adventure, located in Bessemer, Alabama. It was a great place to have fun, especially for the kids. One half of the park consisted of rides, and the other half was a water park. Our boys were really young, and like most kids their age, they enjoyed roller coaster rides, and they also enjoyed swimming.

So, one summer, the four of us went on an Alabama Adventure. We spent a few hours enjoying the rides in the park. My favorite was the log ride. My sons, Jared and Seth, were having the time of their life.

After spending half the day on the rides, we grabbed a bite to eat; then it was off to the water park. This presented a dilemma for me. I wanted my boys to enjoy the water slides, and the lazy river, but I also wanted to keep my heart and my eyes pure in a place where women didn't wear much clothing. My wife and I tried to dress as modestly as we could. She had on a decent outfit, and I had on a muscle shirt and a long pair of swimming trunks. I knew it was risky, but I had a plan. I had already learned the power of meditating on both Christian liberty, and on the purity of Christ. Based on Romans Chapter Seven, my plan was not to go into that environment trying to fight, block, and suppress any desire to look at and to lust after other women. Instead, my plan was to go into that environment focusing on, and concentrating on, verses of Scripture pertaining to my freedom from the law. By doing this, my desires were kept in check the whole time I was there.

In addition, my plan was to focus on verses pertaining to the purity, and the righteousness, and the holiness of Christ. As a result, I was being controlled by His purity. In other words, I kept my eyes on Christ, instead of on the half-dressed women all around me. By using this approach to righteousness, I was able to enjoy a few water slides, and the lazy river, and still have pure eyes and a pure heart at the end of the day. I give all the glory to God! His grace kept me pure. Before I learned about Christian liberty, and Christlikeness, there would have been no way for my heart to remain pure in that type of environment. To God be the glory!

Don't worry, I'm not in the habit of participating in mixed swimming. We rarely go to the beach, and I can't remember the last time I went to a waterpark. As my boys grew older, I thought it wise to limit their time in those types of places.

In conclusion, freedom from the law doesn't mean we can live however we want. Instead, it means that God has given us a new and a much better way of becoming righteous. The old way of trying to fight, block, and suppress sin from entering our minds, through law keeping, doesn't produce lasting victory. Under the Old Covenant, it was all about controlling yourself. However, under the New Covenant, it's all about being controlled by Christ. Instead of fighting with sin, God wants us to focus our minds on the character of Christ, and on the work of Christ. In this way, we can live under God's control instead of being controlled by sin.

13

HOW TO KEEP THE LAW WITHOUT TRYING TO KEEP THE LAW

When I think of what it means to keep the law, the following ideas come to mind. As was previously mentioned, I think of trying to fight, block, and suppress sin when it attempts to enter our minds. I also think of marking a starting date on a calendar to see how long you can go without sinning. Yes, when I think of law keeping, I think of waking up every morning and trying my best not to let myself sin throughout the day. When the Bible tells us that we are not under the law, I believe it means we have been delivered from dealing with sin in the manner I've just described. There is far more to living the Christian life than just trying not to sin. Simply trying not to sin did not work out very well for Paul. Notice the failure, and misery, he endured as a result of trying to conquer sin on his own.

> For that which I am doing, I do not understand; for I am not practicing what I would like to do, but I am doing the very thing I hate. Romans 7:15

> For the good that I wish, I do not do; but I practice the very evil that I do not wish. Romans 7:19

It's hard to determine if Paul is describing his pre-Christian days or a time of frustration he endured after becoming a Christian. Either way, he is describing a scenario that we have all faced at one time or another. We all can relate to trying to overcome a sin, yet being unable to do so. Also, we can relate to doing the very thing we hate and not doing the good we wish to do. Again, we bring a lot of this frustration on ourselves by trying to conquer sin on our own through law keeping.

Thankfully, God has given us a more positive way of dealing with sin and temptation. I believe Paul found that way, because, in Chapter Eight, he is certainly a victorious Christian.

I want to be very clear; God still wants us to fulfill the righteous requirements of the law, according to Romans 8:3,4.

> For what the Law could not do, weak as it was through the flesh, God did: sending His own Son in the likeness of sinful flesh and as an offering for sin, He condemned sin in the flesh, so that the requirement of the Law might be fulfilled in us, who do not walk according to the flesh, but according to the Spirit.

Yes, God wants us to be righteous, but He wants us to become righteous the correct way, as we depend on Him. If we become righteous God's way, then He gets the glory and not us. In this chapter, I want to show you six ways to keep the law without trying to keep the law.

One way to keep the law, without trying to keep the law, is by following the "Golden Rule."

> In everything, therefore, treat people the same way you want them to treat you, for this is the Law and the Prophets. Matthew 7:12

If people would only follow it, this one simple rule could change the whole world. If I understand Jesus here in this passage, He is saying the "Golden Rule" sums up the entire law and the prophets. In fact, the law is based on this one simple rule. In other words, if you follow this rule, you will not commit the sins that are condemned in the law.

The "Golden Rule" is so simple, yet so very powerful. Think about what this rule would eliminate if everyone followed it. There would be no more stealing, or lying, or murder, or adultery, or divorce, or gossip, or bullying, or terrorism. Homelessness, world hunger, prisons, and virtually all wars would be eliminated as well. We could have a truly utopian society.

Another way to keep the law, without trying to keep the law, is to live by faith. To have faith means to believe God's promises with all your heart. Abraham displayed this kind of faith when God promised him a son.

> and being fully assured that what He
> had promised, He was able also to
> Perform. Romans 4:21

Are we fully assured of God's ability to keep His promises? As we see from the life of Abraham, true belief will always manifest itself in obedience.

Notice what Paul said in the book of Galatians:

Now that no one is justified by the Law before God is evident; for, "THE RIGHTEOUS MAN SHALL LIVE BY FAITH."

However, the Law is not of faith; on the contrary, HE WHO PRACTICES THEM SHALL LIVE BY THEM.
Galatians 3:11, 12

These verses have implications pertaining to both salvation and sanctification. I'm dealing, primarily, with the latter in this book.

It's one thing to make a sweeping statement saying that we believe the Bible. It's another matter entirely to make a conscious effort to believe God's promises in the heat of battle. For instance, if you are being tormented by worry, doubt, and fear, you have two options. First, you can try to fight, block, and suppress those unwanted thoughts, or you can believe God's promises. Obviously, option number two is far better. Instead of fighting with your worries, and your fears, try meditating on a wonderful little phrase, such as, "Believe God." Repeat this phrase, silently of course, as you reflect on the promises of God. Repeat it a hundred times, if necessary, until faith takes over and worry dissipates. This is how you make a conscious effort to believe God when temptation is bearing down upon you.

For example, let's use Psalm 23. It's a well- beloved passage. We can read it and quote it all day long. However, it will not bring much peace to us unless we believe every word of it.

Try quoting Psalm 23 the following way:

I believe "The Lord is my shepherd,"

I believe "I shall not want."

I believe "He makes me lie down in green pastures;"

I believe "He leads me beside quiet waters."

I believe "He restores my soul;"

I believe "He guides me in the paths of righteousness for His name's sake."

I believe "Even though I walk through the valley of the shadow of death, I fear no evil, for You are with me;"

I believe "Your rod and Your staff, they comfort me."

> I believe "You prepare a table before
> me in the presence of my enemies;"

> I believe "You have anointed my head
> with oil;"

> I believe "My cup overflows."

> I believe "Surely goodness and
> lovingkindness will follow my all the
> days of my life,"

> I believe "And I will dwell in the house
> of the Lord forever."

If we make a conscious effort to believe the promises of God, day in and day out, we can avoid committing many of the sins which are condemned in both the Old and the New Testaments.

A third way to keep the law, without trying to keep the law, is by having the fruit of the Spirit formed in you.

> But the fruit of the Spirit is love, joy, peace, patience, kindness, goodness, faithfulness, gentleness, self-control; against such things there is no law. Galatians 5:22,23

These are attributes every Christian needs to have. In the Old Testament, the emphasis was on law keeping. However, in the New Testament, the emphasis is on attribute development.

> But if you are led by the Spirit, you
> are not under the Law. Galatians 5:18

How are we to interpret this verse? Well, if you interpret "led by the Spirit" as "Holy Spirit produced attribute development," then the meaning is clear. A person who possesses the attributes mentioned above will automatically make choices that are in harmony with God's moral law. No one has to stand over them telling them not to lie, or steal, or kill, etc. Those wonderful attributes guide every thought, word, and choice we make. It should be noted that we have a responsibility to bear if we are to receive these attributes. The Holy Spirit uses His Word to effect character change in us. Our responsibility is to target, and to meditate on, these attributes in our study of the Scriptures.

Remembering the cross of Christ is another way to keep the law, without trying to keep the law.

> You have been severed from Christ,
> you who are seeking to be justified
> by law; you have fallen from grace.
> Galatians 5:4

There are many ways to attempt to be justified by the law. In the book of Galatians, there were false teachers who tried to include feast days, and circumcision, as a part of the Gospel. This was a grievous error. Those beliefs stemmed from a failure to understand the difference between the two covenants. We are entirely under the New Covenant, and not the Old Covenant. As a result, it would be wrong to bind things like feast days, Sabbath keeping, food laws, and burnt offerings on Christians today.

Another way to attempt to be justified by law keeping is to fight, block, and suppress sin, on our own, while ignoring the character of Christ, and His work on the cross. Surely one can see how the cross is more effective than the law when it comes to restraining fleshly desires. A missionary, by the name of David Brainerd, discovered how the power of the cross can develop righteousness while he was ministering to American Indians. Here is an excerpt from his journal.

"I never got away from Jesus and him crucified. When my people were gripped by this great evangelical doctrine of Christ, and him crucified, I had no need to give them instructions about morality. I found that one followed as the sure and inevitable fruit of the other.... I find my Indians begin to put on the garments of holiness and their common life begins to be sanctified, even in small matters, when they are possessed by the doctrine of Christ, and Him crucified."[1]

In keeping with what we have learned previously, during times of temptation, turning our attention to Calvary is more effective than trying to defeat sin on our own. In this way, the blood of Christ not only cleanses us, but it also gives us victory over sin. If you ever stray from the cross, maybe the following quote will help you find your way back.

"Friends, I beg you to look to the cross. Consider the side pierced by the spear. Gaze at that back ripped to shreds by Roman whips. See the hands and feet penetrated by nails. Give your attention to the sweat and tears of Calvary. Picture the six hours of holy agony the Master endured, because we have offended the Heavenly Father. Think about the precious blood which flowed from His 5 wounds because of our rebellion. Away with our rationalizations! Away with our pitiable excuses! May they be hurled into the depths of the sea. Let us face up to the fact that our sins murdered the Christ. Let us kneel before the Risen Lord, and say God be merciful to us sinners. Then, in humble obedience, let us unreservedly give the remainder of our days to Him, and His purposes."[2] Jimmy Allen.

Loving God and loving people is another way to keep the law without trying to keep the law. You see, our focus should be on loving God more, and loving people more. As a result, our love will grow, thus enabling us to make choices that are in harmony with the moral law of God. Here are a couple of passages which clearly teach this truth:

> …'YOU SHALL LOVE THE LORD YOUR GOD WITH ALL YOUR HEART, AND WITH ALL YOUR SOUL, AND WITH ALL YOUR MIND.' This is the great and foremost commandment. The second is like it, 'YOU SHALL LOVE YOUR NEIGHBOR AS YOURSELF.' On these two commandments depend the whole Law and the Prophets. Matthew 22:37-40

"Owe nothing to anyone except to love one another; for he who loves his neighbor has fulfilled the law. For this, "YOU SHALL NOT COMMIT ADULTERY, YOU SHALL NOT MURDER, YOU SHALL NOT STEAL, YOU SHALL NOT COVET," and if there is any other commandment, it is summed up in this saying, "YOU SHALL LOVE YOUR NEIGHBOR AS YOURSELF." Love does no wrong to a neighbor; love therefore is the fulfillment of the law." Romans 13:8-10

These verses indicate that all the laws are based on either love for God, or love for others. Therefore, if we love God, and if we love people, then we have the law covered. Please tell me, which law would we break if we practice Christian love? I can't think of a single one.

I talked to a man, years ago, who made a statement about his love for God that has stuck with me all these years. We were having a conversation about spiritual matters. He enjoyed discussing the Bible, and so did I. At some point in the discussion we started talking about salvation and whether or not we really felt saved. He said, "I think I'm saved. I love God, and I praise him every day. However, if I don't make it to Heaven, it doesn't matter. I will still praise Him in Hell." I don't think this man was exaggerating. I believe he would continue to love God, and to praise God, even under the worst conditions imaginable. It should be noted that I don't think someone who loves God to that degree has to worry about losing their soul.

There may be some question about how we are to become more loving. I'm glad you asked. In keeping with previous lessons, meditation and prayer are the answers. I remember a turning point in my life, which took place several years ago. I realized I needed more love in my heart. Therefore, I set out on a mission. I devoured every verse I could find on love. I memorized and meditated on these verses until the love of Christ was formed in my heart. I could feel myself becoming more loving by the day. As a result, I found myself sinning less and less. That's the way it works! The more you love, the less you sin! So, anytime you are faced with the temptation to be angry, or to hold a grudge, or to hate someone, please turn your attention to verses on love, and meditate on them until the bad thoughts are gone. Here are some excellent verses that will instill love in your heart:

> Since you have in obedience to the truth purified your souls for a sincere love of the brethren, fervently love one another from the heart. I Peter 1:22

> We love, because He first loved us. I John 4:19

> If someone says, "I love God," and hates his brother, he is a liar; for the one who does not love his brother whom he has seen, cannot love God whom he has not seen. And this commandment we have from Him, that the one who loves God should love his brother also. I John 4:20, 21

> We know love by this, that He laid down His life for us; and we ought to

lay down our lives for the brethren. I
John 3:16

Finally, becoming Christlike is an excellent way to keep the law, without trying to keep the law. One reason the moral law is so difficult to keep is because we aren't as spiritually-minded as we need to be,

> …because the mind set on the flesh
> is hostile toward God; for it does not
> subject itself to the law of God, for it
> is not even able to do so. Romans 8:7

We can develop a spiritual mind by saturating it with the knowledge of Jesus on a continual basis. As we become spiritually-minded, then we can live in harmony with God's law. You see, as we focus on Christ, through the Word, we begin to take on His character which results in closer obedience to the law of God. Again, which of the moral commandments will we break if we live a Christlike existence? I'm not saying we can be perfect by any means. However, sinning less and less and becoming more like Christ are two plausible goals.

This whole book has been building up to this point. Because Christlikeness is so important, the next three chapters will be devoted to this subject. For the Christian, Christlikeness is everything. Please join me as we journey toward Christlikeness. Let's get started.

14

THE THIRD PILLAR OF PURITY: CHRISTLIKENESS

Everything in this book has been leading up to this point. I had to lay the groundwork before discussing the importance of Christlikeness. I cannot over-emphasize the importance of this truth. Christlikeness has changed my life more than I could ever describe in a book. If we miss this truth, I'm afraid we will continue to struggle to live the Christian life. In this chapter, I want to cover a few verses pertaining to Christlikeness. After reviewing these verses, I ask myself, "How could I have missed this truth all those years?" But, better late than never, right? I share these verses with you hoping that you will see the light much sooner than I did. Yes, I hope these Scriptures bless you, and change you, as much as they have me.

Years ago, in a sermon entitled "Christ's People – Imitators of Him," Charles Spurgeon made the following statement:

> "A Christian should be a striking likeness of Jesus Christ... Oh! My brethren, there is nothing that can so advantage you, nothing can so prosper you, so assist you, so make you walk towards Heaven rapidly, so keep your head upwards towards the sky, and your eyes radiant with glory, like the imitation of Jesus Christ."[1]

I do not agree with Charles Spurgeon on several points of theology. However, I agree wholeheartedly with his quote on the imitation of Christ. Outside of Scripture, it's the best quote I've found on this subject. Christlikeness is an often overlooked and neglected Biblical principle. We don't preach on it enough. When I first became a Christian, I wish someone had told me there was more to living the Christian life than just trying not to sin (which seems tantamount to justification by law keeping). If our approach to living for God is simply doing our best not to sin, we will fail, and fail miserably. We need a Christ-centered approach to our walk with the Lord. As Paul said,

> For to me, to live is Christ...
> Philippians 1:21

I can see why Spurgeon preached on imitating Christ, because the concept is so prevalent in Scripture.

> Be imitators of me, just as I also am of
> Christ. I Corinthians 11:1

> Therefore be imitators of God, as
> beloved children. Ephesians 5:1

We have been doing this type of thing all our life, haven't we? We imitate our parents, grandparents, heroes, characters in movies and on TV, sports figures, etc. I even learned how to preach by imitating other preachers. We just need to take this principle and apply it to our relationship with Christ.

According to George Yates, we get our word "mimic" from the Greek word MIMETES. "It means to copy specific characteristics of another person."

> "As imitators of God, Christians are to imitate God's characteristics, and above all His love."[2]

Surely, Thomas A. Kempis had these truths in mind when he made the following statement:

> "There is no higher or more noble work than thinking on Christ, pursuing Christ, desiring the very mind of Christ. To be Christlike is the highest goal of every believer."[3]

The very name we wear, "Christian," emphasizes the importance of Christlikeness. I've heard all my life, and rightly so, that the name Christian means "Christlike," or "A follower of Christ." Either way, the implication of Christlikeness is in the name. If we are going to wear the name Christian, we should strive to be more like Christ in all that we say, and do, and think.

It seems that the theologians of the past had a better understanding of the doctrine of Christlikeness than we do today.

> "I do not want to be like a Paul or any mere man. I want to be like Christ. I want to follow Him only, copy His teachings, drink in His Spirit, and

place my feet in His footprints. Oh, to be more like Christ!"[4] Adoniram Judson

"There are many who preach Christ, but not so many who live Christ. My great aim will be to live Christ." [ibid] Robert Chapman

"Oh, be satisfied with nothing short of a copy of Christ's heart into yours!" [ibid] John Angell James

One passage, which cemented the importance of Christlikeness in my mind, is found in Galatians 4:19.

> My children, with whom I am again
> in labor until Christ is formed in you.

The term "labor" refers to birth pains. I'm not a woman, but I believe that giving birth is one of the most painful experiences a person can endure. Paul used the "pains of childbirth" analogy to describe how badly he wanted the Christians at Galatia to become more Christlike. Paul wanted the attributes of Christ to be formed in each believer, and he wouldn't rest until it happened. We can learn from Paul. We shouldn't just baptize people and then turn them loose to fend for themselves. Instead, we should teach them how to follow Christ.

In 1896, Charles Sheldon wrote a book entitled "In His Steps."[5] Approximately 100 years later, his book inspired the What Would Jesus Do (WWJD) movement. WWJD became the most widely recognized acronym in Christian history. Millions of bracelets, inscribed with WWJD, were sold throughout the country. I remember this movement. I think they were on the right track; however, I wish they had taken it a little further. Instead of asking what Jesus would do in my situation, we should be focused on the person of Christ. When we behold Him, through the Word, Christlike thoughts, words, and actions will naturally appear in our lives. You see, in order to become Christlike, we have to focus on what Christ is like. If you are focused on WIJL (What Is Jesus Like?), then we'll automatically know the answer to the question What Would Jesus Do?

At this point, I hope we agree concerning the importance of Christlikeness. However, there may be some questions about how we can be transformed into His likeness. Hopefully, the last two verses we look at will clear up any confusion you might have. The writer of Hebrews makes a couple of interesting statements relating to our subject.

> Therefore, holy brethren, partakers of a heavenly calling, consider Jesus, the Apostle and High Priest of our confession. Hebrews 3:1

The term "consider," in the previous verse, can be translated to "fix your thoughts on." This rendering will be more helpful in the ensuing discussion.

> Therefore, since we have so great a cloud of witnesses surrounding us, let us also lay aside every encumbrance, and the sin which so easily entangles us, and let us run with endurance the race that is set before us, fixing our eyes on Jesus, the author and perfecter of faith, who for the joy set before Him endured the cross, despising the shame, and has sat down at the right hand of the throne of God. Hebrews 12:1,2

Think about the two phrases "fix your thoughts on Jesus," and "fixing our eyes on Jesus." If we are to become Christlike, it's imperative that we follow these two commands. How do we fix our thoughts on Jesus? We fix our thoughts on Him through the Word! How do we fix our eyes on Jesus? We fix our eyes on Him through the Word, and by realizing His presence in our lives. In other words, by seeking His face, and by keeping His face ever before us. We cannot become Christlike unless we think about Christ on a regular basis.

To illustrate, think about the analogy in Hebrews 12. The writer compares the Christian life to running a race. When running a race, the runner fixes his gaze on the course and on the prize. His concentrated focus is on pushing through to victory. He looks away from all else and zeroes in on winning the race. In the same way, we can't run our race successfully unless we focus our complete attention on the Lord Jesus Christ. Also, the runner's eyes and mind are focused on the prize, just as our eyes and minds are focused on Christ.

Please allow me to use another analogy to illustrate this very important truth. My youngest son is almost old enough to get his driver's license. I've enjoyed teaching him how to drive. However, I'm not sure if he enjoyed being instructed by me. He says I make him nervous, and he can drive better without me in the car.

Oh well. That's neither here nor there. Here's the point: When meeting a vehicle on a two-lane road, especially at night, I taught both of my boys to focus on the white line on the right side of the road. This seems to be the prudent thing to do. It definitely wouldn't be safe to look into the headlights of the oncoming vehicles as they pass by. No, I told them to keep their eyes on the white line until the oncoming car passes. This is exactly how we are to handle temptations. When you meet a temptation, you shouldn't stare at it any more than you should stare at the headlights of an automobile you're meeting. When temptation drives by, stare, gaze, focus, and concentrate on Jesus until it passes.

Actually, there are many things in life that require our focus, concentration, and attention. For instance, when we are driving a nail, we had better be staring at the nail instead of the distractions around us. Therefore, we should focus on Jesus like a carpenter does a nail. In the game of baseball, a player must stare, focus, and gaze at the ball, if he wants to hit it. In the same way, we should fix our eyes on Jesus like a batter in a baseball game. When shooting a gun, you have to aim at the target while looking away from everything else. Becoming Christlike is very similar. We have to look away from everything else and zero in completely on Jesus Christ, through the Word.

We've looked at a few verses about the importance of Christlikeness. There are others. In the next chapter, we'll examine how Christ is our example. These truths are life-changing. I pray that the desire to be Christlike will grip you to the very core of your being.

Christlikeness must be our goal each and every day. I have a long way to go in order to become like Christ, but by the grace of God I'm more like Him than I once was. If you aren't fixing your thoughts upon Jesus, please don't delay another minute. In keeping with the theme of this book, to be pure and to be Christlike are one and the same. Nothing will purify you more than keeping Jesus in your heart. Remember, keeping Jesus in your heart will keep sin out of your life.

15

THE EXAMPLE OF CHRIST

We've had the answer to our struggles with sin available to us this whole time. It's been right under our noses. Actually, we've been singing a song, for many years, that contains the cure for our wicked ways. I've been singing this song in church since I was a little boy. Unfortunately, the full meaning of the song didn't dawn on me until I was well into adulthood. The song "O To Be Like Thee" sums up what I'm saying in these two chapters. Here are the lyrics:

> O to be like Thee! Blessed Redeemer:
> This is my constant longing and
> prayer; Gladly I'll forfeit all of earth's

treasures, Jesus, Thy perfect likeness to wear.

O to be like Thee! Full of compassion, loving, forgiving, tender and kind, helping the helpless, cheering the fainting, seeking the wand'ring sinner to find.

O to be like Thee! Lowly in spirit, Holy and harmless, patient and brave; meekly enduring cruel reproaches, willing to suffer, others to save.

O to be like Thee! Lord, I am coming, now to receive th'anointing divine; All that I am and have I am bringing; Lord, from this moment all shall be Thine.

Chorus:

O to be like Thee! O to be like Thee! Blessed Redeemer, pure as Thou art; come in Thy sweetness, come in Thy fullness, stamp Thine own image deep on my heart.[1]

This song says it all! I thank God for this wonderful song! May we all sing it, believe it, and live it.

The previously mentioned song, in essence, tells us to follow the example(s) of Christ. I do want to point out that following His example is not optional, and it's not a suggestion. Instead, it is a command.

> For you have been called for this
> purpose, since Christ also suffered for
> you, leaving you an example for you
> to follow in His steps, I Peter 2:21

I want to be very clear. We are not saved by following the example of Christ. We are saved by the blood of Christ when we respond to Him with an obedient faith. However, focusing on and following the example of Christ is what transforms us into His image.

I can see God's infinite wisdom in this command. Learning by example is one of the best ways to learn. In every math textbook, before the problems are given, the students are given some helpful examples to go by. In the same way, in nearly every situation we will face, Christ has left us an example to follow. We have a choice; we can do our own thing, or we can follow the example of Christ.

The word "example," in this verse, makes for an interesting study. Our English word "example" comes from the Greek word "upogrammov," which has a couple of different meanings. It can mean, "A writing copy, including all the letters of the alphabet, given to beginners, as an aid in learning to draw them." Or, it can mean, "An example set before one, an underwriting, i.e. a copy for imitation (figuratively), used one time in Scripture."[2] Peter borrows this term from the world of education. School children would often trace the letters of the alphabet in order to improve their writing skills. In context, Peter is referring to how the Christian is to endure suffering. However, since the word "example" is plural, this exhortation would apply to all of His examples. So, what does all of this mean? The implications of this word are astounding. I will let these next two quotes speak for themselves.

> "As a child traces letters on a page, so the Christian traces the path of Christ."[3]

> "The pattern for Christian living is Christ Himself, the one by whom every believer is to trace his life."[4]

The word "steps" is also enlightening. It comes from "icnov," meaning "A footprint, track, footstep; In the NT, metaph.—of imitating the example of anyone."[2] When I was a young child, I remember working with my father, and my grandfather, in the garden. When they plowed the ground with the tiller, they would leave a set of footprints behind. I enjoyed trying to step where their feet had been. When I was successful, there would be only one set of footprints. The examples of Christ are like footprints, or tracks, to follow. If we successfully follow His example(s), there will only be a single set of footprints in our life, namely His.

There may be some question about where the Holy Spirit fits into this discussion. Well, to state the obvious, the Bible tells us that both Christ and the Holy Spirit indwell the believer. Remember, the Holy Spirit is a being. He's not an "it." He has the same attributes as Christ. In fact, He is referred to as "The Spirit of Christ," in Romans Chapter 8. He is the Promised Paraclete, He is our Helper, and He wants to control our life. The Holy Spirit is given to us for many purposes. But here, I will focus on just one.

> But we all, with unveiled face, beholding as in a mirror the glory of the Lord, are being transformed into the same image from glory to glory, just as from the Lord, the Spirit. II Corinthians 3:18

According to this verse, the Holy Spirit is in our life to make us more Christlike! Now, if you ask me to explain how all of that works, I will say, "That's like asking me to explain how God created the world in six days." I believe He did, but I can't explain the mechanics behind the creation. You see, I don't have to be able to explain every detail pertaining to how the Holy Spirit operates in our lives in order to benefit from His help. In a similar way, a person may not even know how to pump gasoline, yet they still benefit from driving their car, because it carries them where they need to go. No, I can't fully explain how the Holy Spirit indwells within us, or how He works in our lives, but I do know what my responsibility is. My responsibility is to focus on Christ, through the Word. As a result, the Holy Spirit controls my life and transforms me into a Christlike person.

Following the footprints of Jesus is similar to Peter's experience of walking on the water. As far as we know, there have only been two people in history who have walked on water. Peter was one and Jesus was the other. Peter is to be commended for stepping out of the boat onto the storm-tossed sea. As long as Peter kept his eyes on Jesus he stayed above the water. Notice what happened when he took his eyes off of Jesus.

> But seeing the wind, he became frightened, and beginning to sink, he

cried out, "Lord, save me!" Matthew 14:30

Our experience is similar to Peter's. As long as we stay focused on Christ, we live a victorious Christian life. When we take our eyes off of Christ, we get that sinking feeling and sin begins to defeat us. The challenge is to keep the example(s) of Christ ever before us.

In order to be pure, we should focus on examples of Christ's purity. Here are two excellent examples of the purity of Christ.

> WHO COMMITTED NO SIN, NOR WAS ANY DECEIT FOUND IN HIS MOUTH; I Peter 2:22

> Jesus …. Has been tempted in all things as we are, yet without sin. Hebrews 4:15

It goes without saying that we can never be as pure as Christ. He was sinless and perfect in every way. Remember, the goal is to be controlled by His purity, and His righteousness, and His holiness. It has to be His purity controlling us instead of us producing our own righteousness. Living the Christian life is not about controlling yourself. Instead, it's about Christ controlling you! Everyone is controlled by something. We are controlled by whatever, or whomever, we fix our minds upon. For instance, if you focus on your problems, then worry will control you. If you focus on your fears, fear will control you. If you focus on fleshly desires, those desires will control you.

On the other hand, if you focus on, and concentrate on, Jesus, through the Word, then Christ will be in control of your heart, and mind, and life. This is where meditation comes in. By way of review, meditation is when we believe, repeat, and reflect on the meaning of a passage of Scripture. If we believe, repeat, and reflect on the two verses above, then Christ's purity will hold sway over our minds. His purity will be formed in us. Please keep this in mind. We do not meditate on these verses for the purpose of suppressing sin. Instead, we meditate on verses about the purity of Christ in order to be filled with His righteousness.

It's also good to meditate on the phrase, "not I, but Christ lives in me," along with the verses listed above. What if unwanted thoughts try to enter our minds? If that happens, we shift our meditation to verses about our freedom from the law. This should kill those desires, thus enabling us to focus clearly on the purity of Christ. I can't tell you how often to repeat and reflect on these verses. I would recommend doing it as often as necessary.

In order to be humble, we need to focus on the example of Christ's humility.

> Being found in appearance as a man, He humbled Himself by becoming obedient to the point of death, even death on a cross. Philippians 2:8

> Take My yoke upon you and learn from Me, for I am gentle and humble in heart, and YOU WILL FIND REST FOR YOUR SOULS. Matthew 11:29

When pride raises its ugly head, we should immediately go to verses like these. Or, if it's hard to remember the entire verse, there is also power in repeating phrases like "Christ is humble," and "Christ is pure." In essence, that is the message of the preceding verses.

J. R. Caldwell made the following statement:

> "I find that the greatest hindrance to the Gospel, and the greatest hindrance to many precious truths taking effect in the hearts and consciences of unbelievers is the Un-Christlike lives of those who profess the truth…"[5]

Our foolish pride may drive someone away from the Lord. This is why we need to be filled with the humility of Christ. Instead of trying to fight, block, and suppress prideful impulses, shift your focus to examples of Christ's humility. If you meditate on Christ's humility long enough, I promise, His humility will be formed in you, thus off-setting the sin of pride in your life.

In order to become more forgiving, go to the examples of Christ's forgiving nature. Perhaps the greatest example of Christ's forgiving spirit is found in the following verse.

> "…. Father, forgive them; for they do not know what they are doing." Luke 23:34

As you concentrate on this example, the sins of anger, bitterness, and hatred will be kept at bay.

President Ronald Reagan displayed a Christlike, gracious, and forgiving spirit after being shot by a would-be assassin. Edward K. Rowell shares the following story:

> In 1981, after being shot, Ronald Reagan's attitude made a lasting impression on his daughter, Patti Davis.
>
> "The following day, my father said he knew his physical healing was directly dependent on his ability to forgive

John Hinckley. By showing me that forgiveness is the key to everything, including physical health and healing, he gave me an example of Christlike thinking."[6]

As the forgiving attitude of Christ is formed in us, we will be able to forgive in such a way that we once thought was impossible.

I would like to recommend one other verse pertaining to forgiveness. This verse has been near and dear to my heart for many years. This verse keeps anger, bitterness, resentment, and hatred at bay every time I turn to it.

> And be kind to one another, tenderhearted, forgiving each other, just as God in Christ also has forgiven you. Ephesians 4:32

Several years ago, I remember being tempted to dwell on a situation in which I felt like I was mistreated. I didn't want to have an unforgiving spirit. I didn't want to become angry or bitter, so I latched onto this verse and repeated it, in my mind, until the victory was won. That's how powerful this verse is. Nothing is more Christlike than forgiving others.

In order to become more loving, turn to examples of Christ's love.

> A new commandment I give to you, that you love one another, even as I have loved you, that you also love one another. By this all men will know that you are my disciples, if you have love for one another. John13:34, 35

Christ gave us an example of pure, unconditional, and sacrificial love. We will be able to love people in a similar way if we meditate on His great example. If I'm having a hard time loving someone, I just remind myself of the love that Christ has for that person.

> But we do see Him who has been made for a little while lower than the angels, namely Jesus, because of the suffering of death crowned with glory and honor, that by the grace of God He might taste death for everyone. Hebrews 2:9

Christ loved humanity to the extent that He died for everyone. Remember, that person you are having a hard time loving is included in the scope of "everyone." If you meditate on the phrase, "Jesus tasted death for everyone," the love of Christ will fill your heart and enable you to love the unlovable.

There are other attributes we need to have as Christians, such as kindness, compassion, joy, courage, a non-materialistic mindset, a heart for soul winning, honesty, and patience. It's just a matter of finding verses where Christ displayed these attributes. When we find those verses, we focus, concentrate, repeat, and reflect on them until we come under His control. Carole Mayhall shared a story that illustrates what God is trying to do in our lives.

"A sculptor once fashioned a magnificent lion out of solid stone. When asked how he had accomplished such a wonderful masterpiece, he replied, 'It was easy. All I did was to chip away everything that didn't look like a lion.'"

All God does is chip away everything in our lives that doesn't look like Christ!"[7]

In conclusion, focusing on the examples of Christ will lead you to be controlled by the Spirit of Christ, which will inevitably make you Christlike. I leave you with these two thoughts as I have outlined them in my own sermons:

> *The more you think about Jesus, the more you will act like Jesus.*

*The more like Jesus you become, the less
of a sinner you will be.*

I pray that Christ will stamp His own image deep
on your heart.

16

PUT ON CHRIST

And that, Knowing the time, that now it is high time to awake out of sleep: for now is our salvation nearer than when we believed. The night is far spent, the day is at hand: let us therefore cast off the works of darkness, and let us put on the armour of light. Let us walk honestly, as in the day; not in rioting and drunkenness, not in chambering and wantonness, not in strife and envying. But put ye on the Lord Jesus Christ, and make

not provision for the flesh, to fulfil the
lusts thereof. Romans 13:11-14 KJV

In this passage, Paul gives the church a wakeup call. He is trying to motivate us to live with a sense of urgency, because time is running out on this old world. Have you ever noticed the sense of urgency a football team, or a basketball team, has when it's late in the game and the score is close? There's no lollygagging around in that situation. Everyone is giving maximum effort, and they are playing with a sense of urgency. We need to have that same sense of urgency in the church. There is way too much lollygagging among Christians, which is sad, because the clock is ticking.

I like the phrase "High time," as it is used in this passage. You don't hear that phrase much anymore. I think it's high time to wake up and apply the four pillars of purity to our lives. It's high time that we study our Bibles and meditate on what we have read. It's high time that we take a closer look at Christian liberty, because our victory over sin depends on it. It's high time that we take Christlikeness seriously, and it's certainly high time to pray. In our passage, the phrase "high time" applies to everything that follows it. God wants to see a sense of urgency as we cast off the works of darkness, and as we put on the armor of light. God doesn't want us to waste any time when it comes to living honest lives, and putting off drunkenness, as well as the other sins listed in the text. The phrase "high time" would certainly apply to putting on the Lord Jesus Christ and making no provision for the flesh.

Yes, it's high time to put on Christ, but first, we need to understand what it means to put on someone. We may have to do a little research to better understand this concept because the idea is not very prevalent in our society today. To help us understand this commandment, I want to go back in time and share what a preacher wrote on this subject during the 1800's. His name was J. W. McGarvey. When I read his take on this verse, I felt like I had been in the mind of a genius. Here is what he wrote:

> Kypke's researches reveal the fact that this bold figure of speech, so little used by us, was very familiar to the writers who were read by those of Paul's day. If a man chose any hero or teacher as an example for his life, or as an object for his imitation, he was said to 'put on' that hero or teacher…. Lucian speaks of one 'having put on Pythagoras,' meaning that to the fullest extent he accepted the great mathematician as his teacher and guide…. "The mode

of speech itself," says Clark, "is taken from the custom of stage players: they assumed the name and garments of the person whose character they were to act, and endeavored as closely as possible to imitate him in their spirit, words and actions...." The initial step by which we put on Christ is by being baptized into him. This great truth Paul had revealed only a few months before he wrote to the Romans (Galatians 3:27). Only after the inward change wrought by being born of the water and of the Spirit (John 3:5, Ephesians 5:26, Titus 3:5) are we capable of making the vesture of our outward conduct such that men may see Him and not ourselves in our daily life."[1]

The preceding quote was a splendid interpretation of the passage under consideration. The idea of putting on someone is foreign to us. However, as McGarvey said, it was very familiar to the original recipients of the New Testament. McGarvey's commentary sets forth three analogies to help us understand what it means to put on Christ: as a hero, an actor, and outer clothing.

We may not understand how to put on someone, but we can certainly relate to having a hero. We all have heroes. When I was young, my heroes came from comic books, or sports, or the movie screen. As I've gotten older, my heroes have changed. I've come to realize that the people who help others and exemplify righteousness, while impacting the world for Christ, are the true heroes. Of course, Christ should be everyone's hero. He is the One True Super Hero! He is the greatest hero of all because He is the Savior of the world. When someone is your hero, you study their life, and you follow their example by imitating them. Therefore, when Christ becomes your greatest hero, the one you accept as teacher and guide, then you can say that you have put on Christ.

We may have a hard time understanding how to put on someone, but we can understand what it means to be an actor in a play, or on TV, or in the movies. I think what actors do is amazing. I don't know how they do it. An actor has to identify closely with the character he or she is portraying. Actors also have to look, talk, walk, and sound like the person they are pretending to be. This is serious work. Some actors may have to lose a lot of weight, or even gain weight, to present a realistic portrayal of their character. They may also spend long hours memorizing their lines. Some actors resemble their real-life counterparts so closely that you can barely tell the difference. The challenge for us is to study the life of Christ as intensely as an actor studies his character. Therefore, when you closely identify with Jesus by trying to walk, talk, and act like him, in your spirit, in your words, and in your actions, then you have put on Christ. Also, if you are memorizing his words, like an actor memorizes his lines, you have put on Christ.

Whether you're talking about having a hero, or portraying a character in a movie, there is one thing both situations have in common. If you have a hero, that hero is on your mind a lot. Also, if you're an actor, the person you are emulating has to be on your mind constantly. To those of you who are struggling to live the Christian life, please let me ask you a question. How often do you think about Jesus throughout the day? If you answered never, seldom, or very little, well, therein lies the problem. There's a beautiful song, recorded by Willie Nelson, Elvis Presley, and others, entitled "Always on my mind." I'm here to tell you that the secret to living the Christian life is to have Jesus always on your mind. When we get to Judgment Day, may it be said of us that Jesus was always on our minds. The best way to keep sin off your mind is to keep Jesus on your mind. Of course, this is accomplished through the Word.

The third analogy to help us understand what it means to put on Christ is the idea of putting on clothing. We can relate to that, can't we? We have our Sunday clothes, our work clothes, and our everyday clothes. You wouldn't leave your house without first putting on your clothes, would you? Therefore, we shouldn't leave the house without first putting on Christ. Clothes are worn on the outside and are visible to everyone. Surely this represents the outward Christlike conduct of the believer. When we are clothed with Christ, the change in our life will be as visible as the clothing we wear. To be clothed with Christ, we must have the attitude of John the Baptist when he said these words about Jesus:

> "He must increase, but I must decrease." John 3:30

Less of self and more of Christ is the idea behind being clothed with Christ. Therefore, if you are clothed with the righteousness of Christ, then you have put on Christ.

Just so you'll know that I didn't dream up this doctrine of Christlikeness, I want to refer to a few other verses pertaining to this subject. I wanted this book to be a fairly exhaustive study of the doctrine of Christlikeness. Here are a few verses we haven't discussed yet.

> More than that, I count all things to be loss in view of the surpassing value of knowing Christ Jesus my Lord, for whom I have suffered the loss of all

things, and count them but rubbish in order that I may gain Christ, and may be found in Him, not having a righteousness of my own derived from the Law, but that which is through faith in Christ, the righteousness which comes from God on the basis of faith, that I may know Him, and the power of His resurrection and the fellowship of His sufferings, being conformed to His death; in order that I may attain to the resurrection from the dead. Philippians 3:9-11

In this passage, Paul emphasizes the importance of knowing Christ. Knowing Christ involves both factual and experiential knowledge of Him. Many people can state facts about Christ, but they don't know Him, because they have no desire to love Him or to be like Him. Knowing Christ inevitably leads to Christlikeness and a deeper love for the Savior.

The preceding passage also teaches the importance of having the righteousness of Christ in our lives, both legally and actually, as opposed to producing our own righteousness. For instance, when it comes to purity, we aren't trying to establish our own purity using our own power. Instead, we want to take on Christ's purity. We also want to take on His humility, His love, His courage, etc. It has to be His righteousness controlling us; hence the phrase "put on Christ."

Avon Malone, in his book Press to the Prize, had an interesting take on this passage.

> "' Not having a righteousness of mine own...' (v.9) introduces a way of being right with God that is beyond the sphere of law and self-effort."[2]

I say amen to his words. That is precisely the message I've been trying to explain in the previous five chapters!

Please allow me to address preachers and counselors for a moment. When a person enters your office asking for your help and guidance, because he or she is struggling with a particular sin, please keep in mind that this person is more than likely trying to keep a law. In other words, your client is trying to suppress a sin on his/her own, separate and apart from the strength Christ provides. I understand exactly how they feel and what they are trying to do. It's very commendable that these people are seeking victory over sin. However, instead of trying to keep a law, they need to be taught how to focus on a person, namely Jesus Christ the Son of the Living God. When they learn to focus on Christ, through His Word and presence, keeping that law will be a natural reaction. Basically, teach them to put on Christ, and then victory will come, and strivings will cease.

The Apostle John, in his first epistle, had a lot to say about Christlikeness.

> …the one who says he abides in Him
> ought himself to walk in the same
> manner as He walked. I John 2:6

It's one thing to say that we are a Christian. But our actions need to match our words. We need to live like Jesus lived, by becoming Christlike as we put Him on.

> And everyone who has this hope fixed
> on Him purifies himself, just as He is
> pure. I John 3:3

Here is yet another passage that teaches the doctrine of Christlikeness. Some call it living the Christ-life, or the exchanged life. I've even seen some refer to this subject as a "second blessing." It truly is like being saved all over again once your eyes are opened to the importance of becoming like Christ in all that we say, and do, and think. Call it what you will, but our motto should be, "O to be like Thee, blessed Redeemer."

> By this, love is perfected with us, that
> we may have confidence in the day of
> judgment; because as He is, so also are
> we in this world. I John 4:17

What a wonderful truth we find here! We all seek to have more assurance of our salvation. John is saying that Christlike people can have confidence on judgment day. They shouldn't fear it. Instead, they can look forward to hearing those words, "Well done, thou good and faithful servant."[3] Today, many people are seeking assurance without change. However, we need the true assurance that comes from a changed life.

In conclusion, I want to make one final appeal to convince you of the importance of living a Christlike life, by putting on Christ. The true test of any doctrine is the change it makes in a person's life. I've applied the principles covered in this book for many years. After examining myself to see if Christ lives in me, as we are instructed to do in II Corinthians 13:5, I must conclude that my mind and character have been totally transformed. Christ has changed me and made me better than I once was. "I once was blind, but now I see," as the song says. I owe it all to His grace and mercy. I believe in these truths so strongly because of the difference they have made in my life. I see no reason why these truths won't change you as well.

Think about this. On Dave Ramsey's radio show, he tries to convince people to commit to debt-free living.[4] To ease the minds of the doubters, he tells them that they can always go back to borrowing money. Using the same logic, I remind you that you can always go back to the approach you have now. If meditating on Christ, and Christian liberty, while praying for Christlikeness doesn't improve your walk with the Lord, then, by all means go back to whatever approach to Christian living you have now. Although, if your approach is unscriptural, I would never recommend that you return to it. I would also say that any approach to Christian living should involve Christlikeness in some way, form, or fashion. You have nothing to lose and everything to gain by living a Christlike life. You will be glad you did, and most importantly, God will too.

17

THE FOURTH PILLAR OF PURITY: PRAYER

"Satan dreads nothing but prayer.... The one concern of the Devil is to keep the saints from prayer. He fears nothing from prayerless studies, prayerless work, prayerless religion. He laughs at our toil, mocks at our wisdom, but trembles when we pray."[1] Samuel Chadwick

We can't discuss Christlikeness without mentioning prayer. Christ is the greatest example of a holy, praying, man of God that we have. E. M. Bounds said, "Christ was the greatest of pray-ers because He was the holiest of men."[1] Therefore, Christlike living involves Christlike praying.

Let's take a look at the prayer life of Jesus. Let's investigate how He prayed. First, apparently Christ would begin His day with a prayer, and He would usually pray in a solitary place.

> And in the early morning, while it was still dark, He arose and went out and departed to a lonely place, and was praying there. Mark 1:35

Beginning our day with prayer is far more important than beginning our day with a cup of coffee. Morning prayer sets the tone for the rest of the day. If we aren't careful we can let an entire day slip away without praying a single prayer. We also need to spend time alone in devotion to God.

Secondly, Christ prayed and gave thanks before meals.

> ...and He took the seven loaves and the fish; and giving thanks, He broke them and started giving them to the disciples, and the disciples in turn, to the multitudes. Matthew 15:36

This is one of the things that separates us from the animals. Instead of tearing into our meals like an animal, let's give thanks for our meals like Christ did. Millions of people around the world starve to death each year. Let's not take our meals for granted.

Third, Christ prayed before making major decisions. For example, Luke records Jesus praying before He chose the twelve Apostles. Also, in that same context we read that Jesus spent the entire night in prayer:

> And it was at this time that He went off to the mountain to pray, and He spent the whole night in prayer to God. Luke 6:12

According to Christ's example, prayer is not to be rushed. God is willing to listen no matter how long we talk. Also, bad decisions can be avoided if we pray beforehand. We should never make an important life decision without first praying about it.

Fourth, Jesus prayed at significant moments in His life such as at His baptism and His farewell address to His disciples. The writer of Hebrews gives us insight into how earnestly Christ prayed.

> In the days of His flesh, He offered up both prayers and supplications with loud crying and tears to the One able

to save Him from death, and He was heard because of His piety. Hebrews 5:7

The church needs prayer warriors who will pray earnest, heartfelt, fervent, and believing prayers.

Fifth, Christ prayed for others. He prayed for the sick. He even prayed for his enemies when He was dying on the cross. He also prayed for people who were in spiritual trouble. For instance, He prayed for Peter when he was about to endure an onslaught from the Devil.

"Simon, Simon, behold, Satan has demanded permission to sift you like wheat; but I have prayed for you, that your faith may not fail; and you, when once you have turned again, strengthen your brothers." Luke 22:31, 32

We do a really good job of praying for the sick, but praying for the spiritually ill and for our enemies is often neglected. Like Jesus, and like Paul, much of our prayer life should involve intercessory praying. I submit to you that Peter would not have been able to preach the first Gospel sermon, on the day of Pentecost, had Jesus not prayed for him.

Additionally, Christ prayed for the will of God to be done. He prayed for unity among all believers. He also prayed while suffering in the Garden of Gethsemane. Now that's how praying is done! Remember, He is our example. He is our template. He is the Original and we are the copies of Him. Therefore, let's pattern our prayer life after His.

Down through the years, there have been some great quotes given on the subject of prayer. Here are a couple of them:

> "Prayer moves the hand that moves the world."[1]

> "7 days without prayer makes one weak." Unknown

This quote was on the bulletin board of the church I grew up in. Every time we walked in the building we saw that quote. I don't suppose I'll ever forget it. The saying teaches a powerful truth. Did you know that prayerlessness is a sin? The prophet Samuel certainly believed it was wrong to stop praying.

> "Moreover, as for me, far be it from me that I should sin against the Lord by ceasing to pray for you…" I Samuel 12:23

Are we really any better than the atheists if we cease to pray? There is no way to remain strong if we don't pray on a regular basis.

Another reason to keep praying is that great things happen when we pray. It seems that nearly every great event in the Bible was preceded by prayer. Prayer preceded the glorious exodus of the Israelites from Egypt. In Nehemiah's day, many prayers preceded the building of the wall. Some of the most fervent praying the world has ever known preceded the death, burial, and resurrection of Christ. Prayer preceded the day of Pentecost, when the Spirit was poured out and the glorious body of Christ came into existence. John's prayers preceded the Revelation of Jesus Christ to the seven churches of Asia. The list could go on and on. These great events might not have happened had the people not prayed first. Great things will not happen in our lives, or in our churches, unless we are devoted to prayer.

As Christians, we have the assurance that God will both hear and answer our prayers.

> "And all things you ask in prayer, believing, you shall receive." Matthew 21:22

> FOR THE EYES OF THE LORD ARE UPON THE RIGHTEOUS, AND HIS EARS ATTEND TO

> THEIR PRAYER, BUT THE FACE OF THE LORD IS AGAINST THOSE WHO DO EVIL. I Peter 3:12

> …and whatever we ask we receive from Him, because we keep His commandments and do the things that are pleasing in His sight. I John 3:22

> And this is the confidence which we have before Him, that, if we ask anything according to His will, He hears us. And if we know that He hears us in whatever we ask, we know that we have the requests which we have asked from Him. I John 5:14, 15

Remember, faith is believing that God will perform what He has promised. It's good to make a conscious effort to believe these promises before, during, and after we pray.

David had supreme confidence in God's ability to answer his prayers.

> In the morning, O Lord, you hear my voice; in the morning I lay my requests

before you and wait in expectation.
Psalm 5:3 (NIV)

Do we wait in expectation after we pray? Years ago, I was fishing out on the lake with my uncle Sam. It was hot! We'd been out there for a while, and I hadn't caught anything. I was growing impatient, so I turned to Sam and asked, "Have you gotten any bites yet?" He said, "No, but I'm expecting one any time now." Sure enough, he started reeling those big catfish in. He caught several more fish than I did. That's the power of expectation. Expect God to answer your prayers and He will.

The Lord sure does work in mysterious ways. One day, many years ago, I learned a powerful lesson about prayer as I was riding in my automobile and listening to the radio. On one particular channel, a storyteller shared an amazing tale. The setting of the story was during the 1800's. A mother and her children were traveling by horse and wagon while on a very long journey. Everything was going wrong for this little family. They were having a miserable time! Just when it seemed like things couldn't get any worse for them, they were caught in the middle of a bad rain storm. It was during this time that one of the children made a profound statement. The lady's son said, "I sure am glad we prayed before starting this journey." The mother said, "What do you mean? Everything has gone wrong on this trip!" Her son said,

"Well, if we hadn't prayed it might have snowed!" The situation could always be worse, right? Only God knows how many further catastrophes have been prevented in our lives through prayer.

What I'm about to share with you is nothing short of life changing. I want to leave you with a scripturally-based prayer. I don't know who coined the phrase "Praying the Scriptures," or I would give them credit for it. When you "Pray the Scriptures" you let the Word of God dictate the requests you make before the Heavenly Father. The idea is to take a verse of Scripture and turn it into a prayer. I'm sharing with you a prayer for Christlikeness.

Before I begin, I should qualify a couple of phrases that you will read in this prayer. You will see the phrase "filled with" repeatedly throughout the prayer. The Greek term can mean "to influence."[2] In Ephesians 5:18, Paul talks about being "filled with the Spirit." In context, he is talking about being under the influence of the Spirit, or being controlled by the Spirit, as opposed to being controlled by fermented beverages. I'm using the term "filled with" to indicate "being controlled by." Also, you will see the term "manifested." This word, as used in II Corinthians 4:11, means "Brilliantly Seen."[3] I encourage you to take this prayer and make it your own. Adapt it and improve upon it, if you wish. When you pray this prayer, please don't pray it in a rehearsed or mechanical sort of way. All praying should be faith filled, heartfelt, and done out of love for God.

Dear Father in Heaven, I bow before You thanking you for Your grace, and for Your Mercy, and for Your wonderful love. I'm eternally grateful for Your Son Jesus, and thank You for sending Him to die for our sins. Lord, I humbly beg you to forgive all of my many sins. I pray to be made clean by the blood of Jesus. Father, I pray that my love for You will grow stronger and stronger with every passing second. I pray that my love for people will grow stronger and purer every minute of every day. Please give me peace that passes all understanding, and help me to be positive, optimistic, hopeful, and faith-filled in every situation.

Father, I pray for Christ to be formed in me. I pray to be conformed to the image of Christ. I pray for the life of Christ to be manifested in my body. Please help me to be more like Jesus in all that I say and do and think, as Jesus lives in me and through me. Father, I pray to be filled with your Holy Spirit, and please fill me with all the fullness of Christ. I pray to be filled with the pure love, the unconditional love, and the sacrificial love of Jesus. Please fill me with the purity, and righteousness, and holiness of Christ. Father, I pray to be filled with the meekness and the humility of Christ. Please fill me with the patience and the wisdom of Christ. I pray to be filled with the peace and the joy of Christ. Please fill me with the mind of Christ toward money, and wealth, and riches. I pray to be filled with the trusting heart of Jesus. Please fill me with the forgiving heart of Jesus, and Father, please fill me with the evangelistic zeal and the evangelistic fervor of Jesus.

Heavenly Father, I pray for the power of Christ to rest upon me and upon all Christians everywhere throughout the world. I pray to have a heart that is fixed upon Jesus at all times, and please help me to "Stand fast in the liberty wherewith Christ has made us free."[4] Father, I pray that You will help us to realize that there are lost souls all around us. Please transform us into Christlike, loving, courageous, compassionate, concerned, humble, thankful, joyful, prayerful, faith-filled, peace-filled soul winners, to the praise of Your glory. In Jesus name I humbly pray, Amen.

18

NEVER GIVE UP

Therefore, since we have this ministry, as we have received mercy, we do not lose heart. II Corinthians 4:1

Therefore we do not lose heart, but though our outer man is decaying, yet our inner man is being renewed day by day. II Corinthians 4:16

The Apostle Paul was not one to give up, as the preceding verses indicate. The terms "Lose heart," and "Give up," are synonymous. The fact that Paul never gave up is even more impressive when you consider the trials he endured for the cause of Christ. Sandwiched between the two verses listed above is a detailed description of Paul's trials, and his tribulations.

> We are afflicted in every way, but not crushed; perplexed, but not despairing; persecuted, but not forsaken; struck down, but not destroyed; always carrying about in the body the dying of Jesus, that the life of Jesus also may be manifested in our body. For we who live are constantly being delivered over to death for Jesus' sake, that the life of Jesus also may be manifested in our mortal flesh. II Corinthians 4:8-11

In spite of immense pressure, Paul never lost heart, because he knew God was with him.

Paul had what some call "stick-to-it-ive-ness." I first heard that term while watching a football game on TV. I think the announcer made up a new word, but you get the picture. There was too much at stake for Paul to ever give up. The work he was involved in was way too important for him to "throw in the towel." The same holds true for us. It helps us to "stay the course" when we remind ourselves that, as Christians, we are involved in the greatest work in the history of the world.

Even though most Christians will not face a tenth of the trials that Paul faced, many will still give up. What about you? It's good that you've started living the Christian life. The question is, do you plan on finishing it? Judging by church attendance, and church rolls, we have many starters but far too few finishers. Why? Because we give up too easily. In fact, today, there are some who freely give up what the early Christians, like Paul, died to keep.

As a Christian, you will face disappointment. Never give up! You will be talked about, and criticized, and made fun of, because of your faith. Never give up! You will make mistakes, and you may even fall flat on your face. Never give up! You will have your feelings hurt. Never give up! You may be ignored, neglected, and even forgotten by some of your own brethren. Never give up! You may be persecuted, and your life may be threatened. Never give up! At times, you may feel like your prayers aren't being heard, or answered. Never give up! Experiencing spiritual growth may take a tremendously long time. Never give up! Adversity, trials, and hardships will come our way. Never give up! With God's help, in spite of all these things, we will never lose heart.

I must admit, there have been a few times when I've contemplated quitting the ministry. However, every time I became discouraged, God would prove Himself faithful and pick me up.

On one occasion, I remember being very discouraged. During that time, we were having a Gospel Meeting. Ken Butterworth, of Birmingham, Alabama, was doing the preaching. Brother Ken liked to use charts when he preached. On one particular night, he had a chart with a frog and a crane painted on it. The crane was trying to swallow the frog. The frog was half way in the crane's mouth, but if you looked closely, you could see the frog's hands tightly wrapped around the crane's throat. The frog was squeezing the life out of that old crane. That frog was not going to give up. He wasn't going down without a fight. Ken had a great sermon that night, and it was just what I needed to hear. I told him how much I appreciated it, and I kept pressing onward and upward.

On another occasion, when I was having a difficult time, I was delivering drinks to a Christian school. It had been a rough day, and I needed some encouragement. I didn't have to wait long. As I was making my delivery in the building, I looked up and saw the following verse in a picture frame hanging on the wall.

> "For I know the plans I have for you,"
> declares the Lord, "plans to prosper you
> and not to harm you, plans to give you
> hope and a future."[1] Jeremiah 29:11

God knows exactly what we need, and when we need it. That verse spoke right to my heart, and lifted me up, and gave me the strength to carry on.

On yet another occasion, in my darkest hour, God came through for me again. I went to visit a relative. As we visited, I shared all my troubles with him. At the time, I felt like my situation was hopeless, and I didn't know how I was going to make it another day. My relative was a good listener, so I poured out my heart to him. As we were talking, the front door opened rather quickly. In walks another cousin of mine. Keep this in mind. He has no idea that I'm upset. As soon as he walked in, he said these words, "Jeff, when it looks like you've lost it all, and you haven't got a prayer, Jesus will still be there." What a blessing! My other relative, who was still in the room, said, "Whoa!" God knew I needed to hear those words. My cousin had just been listening to the song "Jesus Will Still be There"[2] on the radio. He felt like saying those words to someone and it just happened to be me, the person who needed to hear them the most. The Providence of God is amazing. That event gave me hope, and it showed me that things would get better, and they did. By the grace of God, I didn't give up, and here I am now writing this book.

Long distance runners experience something called a "Second Wind." I experienced it a few times, back when I used to jog. When you're jogging several miles, at some point you will feel like stopping. When fatigue sets in and you're breathing hard, and your legs and feet are aching, if you keep pressing on you will eventually feel that extra burst of energy called, "The Second Wind." The Bible compares living the Christian life to running a race.[3] In this spiritual race, there will come a time when you feel like quitting. If we persevere, with the Lord's help, we will catch our spiritual second wind. As a Christian, it would be a tragedy to give up when you're so close to catching your "Second Wind."

Ladies, if your husband isn't a Christian, don't give up. I attended a church service one night. While there, I heard the preacher tell this story on himself. This man was not a Christian when he first married, but his wife was a dedicated Christian. On Sunday, she was going to church, with him or without him. Sadly, most of the time she went to church by herself. The man even tried to stop his wife from attending worship services. He tried to keep her from using the car, but she reminded him that she owned half the car, and her half was going to church. So, he came up with another plan. One Sunday morning, as his wife was getting ready to go to church, he entered the room. He asked her to stay home and she refused. Then he said, "I think you love God more than you love me!" His wife looked him in the eye and said, "You may not get anything else right, but you got that right!" Time went on. God prevailed. The man in our story eventually became a Christian, and he even went on to make a preacher. He had a great ministry. He preached over 600 Gospel Meetings, and he influenced thousands of lives for Christ. That's what happens when you don't give up.

Based on the following verses, God wants us to have the qualities of persistence, patience, perseverance, fortitude, resilience, tenacity, diligence, and determination. As a Christian, if you possess these qualities, you will never give up, or give in, or surrender, or quit.

> Therefore, my beloved brethren, be steadfast, immovable, always abounding in the work of the Lord, knowing that your toil is not in vain in the Lord. I Corinthians 15:58

> And let us not lose heart in doing good, for in due time we shall reap if we do not grow weary. Galatians 6:9

> For consider Him who has endured such hostility by sinners against Himself, so that you may not grow weary and lose heart. Hebrews 12:3

> For a righteous man falls seven times, and rises again, but the wicked

stumble in time of calamity. Proverbs 24:16

Several years ago, I came across a poem that strengthens my resolve every time I read it. Actually, this poem was hanging on the wall in my brother's bedroom for many years. I'm sure he placed it on his wall to keep him going when he felt like quitting. It's a good poem to read when you're down and discouraged. The poem is entitled "Don't Quit." It was written many years ago by John Greenleaf.

> When things go wrong, as they sometimes will,
>
> When the road you're trudging seems all uphill,
>
> When funds are low, and debts are high,
>
> And you want to smile, but you have to sigh.
>
> When care is pressing you down a bit,
>
> Rest if you must, but don't you quit….
>
> Often the goal is nearer than
>
> It seems to a faint and faltering man;

Often the struggler has given up,

When he might have captured the victor's cup.

And he learned too late, when the night slipped down

How close he was to the golden crown.

Success is failure turned inside out

The silver tint of the clouds of doubt,

And you can never tell how close you are,

It may be near when it seems afar.

So, stick to the fight when you're hardest hit,

It's when things seem worse that you mustn't quit.[4]

Sometimes, hearing about the persistence of others can inspire us to hang on when the going gets tough. John Wesley wrote something in his journal that we all need to read. Now, please understand, I'm not endorsing everything he taught. However, I do believe in giving credit where credit is due. He was one determined individual, and he never gave up. I applaud his resilience and his fortitude. Here is an excerpt from his journal entries:

> Sunday, A.M., May 5: Preached in St. Anne's. Was asked not to come back anymore. Sunday, P.M., May 5: Preached in St. John's. Deacons said, "Get out and stay out." Sunday, A.M., May 12: Preached in St. Jude's. Can't go back there either. Sunday, A.M., May 19: Preached in St. Somebody Else's. Deacons called a special meeting and said I couldn't return. Sunday, P.M., May 19: Preached on Street. Kicked off street. Sunday, A.M., May 26: Preached in meadow. Chased out of meadow as bull was turned loose during service. Sunday, A.M., June 2: Preached out at the edge of town. Kicked off the highway. Sunday, P.M., June 2: Afternoon, preached in a pasture. Ten thousand people came out to hear me.[5]

Now, perhaps that was a preacher's count, because we do tend to round up. However, since he preached near London, England, it would have been possible to have a crowd that size in attendance.

In this book, we have covered the four pillars of purity: Biblical meditation, Christian liberty, Christlikeness, and prayer. Never give up on meditation because it allows the Word of God to permeate every facet of your being. Never give up on Christian liberty because this truth is designed to weaken your sinful desires. Never give up on Christlikeness because it is your destiny as a Christian.[6] Never give up on prayer, because God is listening, and He will answer.

Well, there you have it. *The Path to Purity*. As you journey down this path, you must never give up, or quit. The path to purity isn't always easy, but it's always worth it, because it's the path that always leads to Heaven. God bless you for reading this book. To God be the glory.

REFERENCES

CHAPTER ONE

A.L. Franks, Editor, "Magnolia Messenger," Kosciusko, MS. Volume 39; Number 1; SPRING, 2017, p. 9. Used by permission.

Proven Men Porn Survey (conducted by Barna Group), located at https://www.Provenmen.org/2014Pornsurvey/. Used by permission.

CHAPTER 2

Luke 18:13

7 Ways Anger Is Ruining Your Health, retrieved from https://www.everydayhealth.com/news/way-anger-ruining-your-health/

Unless otherwise indicated, "Scripture taken from the NEW AMERICAN STANDARD BIBLE, copyright 1960, 1962, 1963, 1968, 1971, 1972, 1973, 1976, 1977, by The Lockman Foundation. Used by permission."

CHAPTER 3

Mel Gibson, "The Passion of the Christ," 2004.

Lynn Camp, 'The Train Story,' Eastern European Mission, Dallas, TX. Used by permission.
CHAPTER 4 Edited and compiled by Frank Charles Thompson, D.D., Ph.D., The Thompson Chain-Reference Bible, B.B Kirkbride Bible Company, Inc., Indianapolis, IN1993, p 609.

CHAPTER 5

Alex Kendrick, Stephen Kendrick, Eric Wilson, "Facing the Giants," Harper Collins, September 29, 2006 USA.

Fannie E. C. Davison, 'Purer in Heart, O God," 1877, Public Domain.

CHAPTER 6

Excerpt from *750 Engaging Illustrations for Preachers, Teachers, and Writers* by Craig Brian Larson, copyright 1993, 1996, 1998. Used by permission of Baker Books, a division of Baker Publishing Group.

James Strong, STRONG'S EXHAUSTIVE CONCORDANCE OF THE BIBLE, Hendrickson Publishers, Peabody, MA, p 820.

The Dave Ramsey Show, Nashville Tennessee.

CHAPTER 7

1. "National Treasure," November 19, 2004 USA.

Rutgers School of Arts and Sciences, Thomas A. Edison Papers, The Edisonian-Volume 9 Fall 2012, accessed July 13, 2018. Retrieved from http://www.edison.rutgers.edu/newsletter9.html Used by permission.

Merriam-Webster online dictionary, accessed July 13, 2018. Retrieved from http://www.merriam-webster.com/dictionary/self-flagellation

CHAPTER 8

History of the Restoration Movement, accessed on Aug. 16, 2018. Retrieved from https://www.therestorationmovement.com/_states/Kentucky/smith,johnhtm Used by permission.

CHAPTER 9

John F. MacArthur Jr., Why Believe the Bible (Glendale, CA: Regal Books, 1980), 95.

The One Year Bible, Tyndale House Publishers, Wheaton, Il. 1986.

CHAPTER 10

Thomas Brooks, Public Domain.

James Strong, STRONG'S EXHAUSTIVE CONCORDANCE OF THE BIBLE, Hendrickson Publishers, Peabody, MA, p 668.

Thomas Watson, Gleanings from Thomas Watson, Soli Deo Gloria Publications, Morgan, PA, 1995, 33.

Andrew Murray quote – Public Domain.

Thomas Watson, retrieved from https://gracequotes. org/topic/bible-meditation/ Used by permission.

CHAPTER 12

Accessed on 5/5/2018, Retrieved from: www.greatblackheroes.com/sports/hank-aaron/ Used by permission.

CHAPTER 13

Excerpt from 1500 Illustrations for Biblical Preaching by Michael P. Green, copyright 1982, 1985, 1989. Used by permission of Baker Books, a division of Baker Publishing Group.

The quote is from Jimmy Allen, retired professor at Harding University in Searcy, Arkansas. Used by permission.

CHAPTER 14

Spurgeon, Charles. "Christ's People-Imitators of Him." Blue Letter Bible. 18 Apr. 2001. Web. 15 Oct. 2018. https://www.blueletterbible.org/comm/spurgeon_charles/sermons/0021.cfm delivered Apr. 29, 1855. Used by permission.

George Yates, "Be Imitators," Accessed on: July 24, 2018. Retrieved from https://www.sermoncentral.com/sermons/be-imitators-george-yates-sermon-on-character-96137?page=1&wc=800 Used by permission.

Thomas A. Kempis, THE IMITATION OF CHRIST, Public Domain.

Retrieved from: https://gracequotes.org/?topic=christ-likeness&author-quote=&s= Used by permission.

Charles Sheldon, In His Steps, Chicago Advance, 1896.

CHAPTER 15

Thomas O. Chisholm, "O to Be Like Thee!" 1897, Public Domain.

Byron Sherman, "Christian Governance Work 3," accessed July 24, 2018, Retrieved from https://www.sermoncentral.com/sermons/Christian-governance-work-3-byron-sherman-on-work-208635?page=2&wc=800 Sources used:

1) Thayer's Greek-English Lexicon of the New Testament (1889);

2) Strong's-Hebrew Chaldee and Greek English Lexicons (1890) Used by permission.

Arnie Silva, "For Even Hereunto Were Ye Called," Accessed July 24, 2018, Retrieved from hiparnold.blogspot.com/2015/08/for-even-hereunto-were-ye-called.html

John MacArthur, Ephesians MacArthur New Testament Commentary, The Moody Bible Institute, Chicago, IL 1986, 196.

Walter B. knight, Knight's Master Book of 4,000 Illustrations, William B. Eerdmans Publishing Company, Grand Rapids, MI 1956, 70.

Excerpt from 1001 Quotes, Illustrations, and Humorous Stories for Preachers, Teachers, and Writers by Edward K. Rowell, copyright 1996, 1997. Used by permission of Baker Books, a division of Baker Publishing Group.

Carole Mayhall, Filled to Overflowing, (Colorado Springs: Navpress, 1984), 97-107.

CHAPTER 16

J. W. McGarvey, LL.D., and Philip Y. Pendleton, A.M., Commentary on Thessalonians, Corinthians, Galatians and Romans, Gospel Light Publishing Company, Delight, Arkansas, p 522. Used by permission.

Avon Malone, Press to the Prize Studies in Philippians, 20th Century Christian, Nashville, TN, 1991, p 82. Used by permission.

Matthew 25:23

The Dave Ramsey Show, Nashville, TN.

CHAPTER 17

E. M. Bounds, compiled and condensed by Leonard Ravenhill, A Treasury of Prayer: The Best of E.M. Bounds, Broadstreet Publishing Group, LLC, Racine, WI 1989, 199, 195. Used by permission.

James Strong, STRONG'S EXHAUSTIVE CONCORDANCE OF THE BIBLE, Hendrickson Publishers, Peabody MA, 349.

Dr. Spiros Zodhiates, Illustrations of Bible Truths, AMG Publishers, Chattanooga, TN, copyright 1998, 305. Used by permission.

Galatians 5:1

CHAPTER 18

Scripture taken from the HOLY BIBLE, NEW INTERNATIONAL VERSION. Copyright 1973, 1978, 1984 by International Bible Society. Used by permission of Zondervan Publishing House. All rights reserved.

Point of Grace, "Jesus Will Still Be There," 1993.

Hebrews 12:1

John Greenleaf, "Don't Quit," Public Domain.

Grace Quotes, 2015. Accessed on July 24th, 2018. Retrieved from https://gracequotes.org/author-quote/ john-wesley/ Used by permission.

Romans 8:29, I John 3:2

www.ingramcontent.com/pod-product-compliance
Lightning Source LLC
Chambersburg PA
CBHW051802050726
47598CB00006B/2389